STO

ALLEN COUNTY PUBLIC LIBRARY

ACPL ITEM

3 1833 0034

DISCARDED

P9-ELH-640

MAR 14 1956

DEC 1 9 '55

DEC 1 9 '56

How to Make
CHURCH SCHOOL
EQUIPMENT

It's Easier than You Think!

by
THELMA ADAIR
and
ELIZABETH McCORT

Philadelphia
THE WESTMINSTER PRESS

COPYRIGHT, MCMLV, BY W. L. JENKINS

All rights reserved--no part of this book may be reproduced in
any form without permission in writing from the publisher, except
by a reviewer who wishes to quote brief passages in connection
with a review in magazine or newspaper.

Library of Congress Catalog Card Number: 55-7707

Printed in the United States of America

This volume is dedicated
to
all the creative teachers
in our church schools
who have done new and wonderful things
with what they have

926080

CONTENTS

The experiences on which this book is based
can be of help to
the rural, one-room church;
the small, crowded urban church;
the church meeting "almost anywhere";
the church with big, "barny" rooms for
small groups
and any others facing problems
that have to do with time, space, and equipment

CHAPTER

I

HOW IT ALL BEGAN

Have you ever heard these words--or similar ones?
"There just isn't enough room."
"How can I do these things in the time I have?"
"We spend most of the hour just moving from here to
   there!"
"You can't do this kind of teaching without things to work
   with and we can't afford fancy equipment."
"We haven't any place to put it, even if we had it!"
"How can we do anything but lecture when there's another
   class just six feet away?"
"I haven't time to plan all this stuff!"
"It's hard enough just to keep my boys quiet!"

It was to face and solve such problems that a special laboratory
school went into action for two successive years in connection with
our School of the South . (Presbyterian, U.S.A., Summer Training
School , Maryville College, Maryville, Tenn., June, 1953, 1954 .
Under the auspices of the Children's Work Department of the Board
of Christian Education.) It was agreed that if we could get results
in what is perhaps the most limited situation--a small one-room
church--we would make discoveries that would be useful not only
in that particular place but in many others equally baffling in
somewhat different ways.

We wanted to demonstrate to the satisfaction of the most skepti-
cal that it is possible in such a room to have a graded church school,
and in it to use a variety of good teaching methods, particularly
those that center in activities in which the pupils share--what is
sometimes called "learning by doing." For it is in regard to this
kind of teaching that the cry most frequently goes up, "We can't
do that!"

The obstacles usually named are:
1. Lack of space .
2. Lack of money for equipment.
3. All age groups in the same room.

4. "Cluttering up" the church sanctuary.
5. Teachers who cannot adapt the lesson plans to the difficulties of their situation.

And we did it! There were two highly successful demonstrations, of three days each, given in the West Maryville Presbyterian Church, which is in a semirural section on the outskirts of Maryville, Tennessee. Although the church actually has a nice basement room, we pretended it was not there, and used only the sanctuary, a room 39' x 28' (diagrams, pages 10, 11). The church (page 6) is on a small, sunny knoll and is surrounded by trees. Its order and cleanliness, the attractive green and cream of the interior (recently painted by some of the members), and the light oak pews made a bright and cheerful setting for our work. The co-operation and interest of the West Maryville people made it possible to key the experiment to their needs rather than to imaginary ones.

We found it entirely possible to house there a completely graded church school; to construct (although most of the group were strictly amateurs with tools!) the necessary equipment, using odds and ends of "scrounged" materials; to make such equipment really sturdy and attractive; to blend it with the setting or remove it easily and quickly; to train relatively inexperienced people to do the job.

The diagram on page 10 is of the church school as it was arranged the first day we visited there. The downstairs room was out of use because it was being painted. There was nothing for any age group in the way of equipment except the pews.

The diagram on page 11 indicates the plan of use we made and carried out. Because of the need for space for observers during the three days of actual demonstration, we did not actually have classes above junior age. The observers in greater number than the class members they replaced, provided all that was needed for testing in the way of numbers, noise, and nuisance! The changes actually made, outside of adding needed equipment, were:

Separating the nursery-kindergarten children from the primary group.
Condensing all other groups into more compact form--not having a class strung out against a wall, as the young people had been.
Planning for a possible "back wall" for each teacher.
Facing the primary and junior groups toward a wall, instead of having them face other groups that might distract them.

In planning our program, we did what we could to cut down distractions caused by routine movements: making the offering a part of worship, having class records taken to the secretary at the close of the class period, and in other ways reducing such interruption to a minimum. To gain time there was, on two of the days, only one carefully planned--and brief!-- period of general assembly, mainly for worship. On one day this was an opening service for all;

on another it was a closing service, making use of certain contributions the department had been asked for. On the third day, it was assumed that in this church, to which family groups came as a whole, the morning church service provided group worship. So on that day there was no general assembly, each group using the additional time to plan some form of worship as part of their own teaching plan. Two of the groups even sang, softly and without accompaniment, and did not even rate a glance from the others!

On each of the days, the nursery-kindergarten spent part of the church school hour outdoors. It would have been entirely possible for other groups to do so.

The basic equipment made was as follows:

For the Nursery-Kindergarten
1. Supply cabinet
2. Folding table
3. Bookrack screen
4. Display cabinet
5. Stools
6. Doll bed
7. Easel for painting
8. Paper rack
9. Wall bag (for small articles)
10. Box (for small treasures)
11. Water can (for washing hands)
12. Chairs--property of church
13. Pew used as table

For the Primary Group
14. Partitioned box for supplies (also used for worship equipment)
15. Supply cabinets
16. Table top (placed on supply cabinets as supports, when in use)
17. Screen (used also as bulletin board)
18. Pads for sitting on floor
19. Pews used for seating and picture display
20. Nail kegs padded for chairs

For the Junior Group
21. Supply cabinet table
22. Supply cabinets (2)
23. Narrow table top (used with cabinets as supports)
24. Chart rack
25. Lapboards
26. Pews used for seating
27. Chair for teacher

Each piece of equipment that was above pew height or that

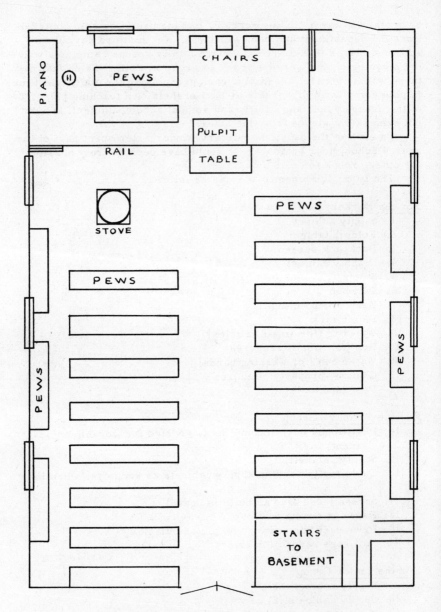

Maryville Church before rearrangement.

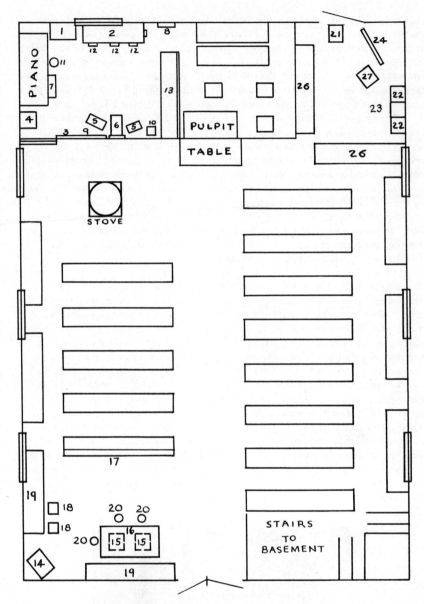

Maryville Church after rearrangement.

11

stood against the walls was painted the same shade of light green as the walls. Each piece that was used near the pews (as benches) or was of pew height (as tables) was stained the light oak of the pews. Incidentally, although we mixed--and even bought--some of the paint and stain used, we found that this would not have been necessary, as there had been some leftovers after painting the church interior that would have been available to us had we done a little searching!

Every piece of equipment was made to fit into a particular space, both when it was in use and when not needed. Each, therefore, during the church service, was either out of the way, inconspicuous, or a real addition to the decorative scheme. Open shelves were turned backward against the wall so a flat surface the color of the wall was in evidence rather than the books, toys, or work materials on the shelves. Only the junior worship table, supply case, and chart rack (all light in weight) had to be carried to a different location, a corner near the back stairs. This was possible because, in our planning, each inch of space was carefully considered, and nothing was made that was not needed for constant use.

The results were sufficiently worth-while, it was felt, to be shared in book form with others facing the same, or similar, problems. But to make very sure of the projected book's possible value, and of the facts presented, the first draft was sent out for reading, checking, and further experimentation. It went to over a hundred interested people across the country, in churches small and large, prosperous and "not so, " in rural, town, and city centers. More than seventy of these were returned, with thoughtful criticisms and many good suggestions--but unanimously expressing approval of the general idea and contents. Because there were so many similarities and duplications in the suggestions, and because in many instances no one knew the original source of an idea, no acknowledgment has been made here to particular people or churches for material used.

Now the book comes to you as, we hope, a useful tool. It will not of itself solve all your problems, but it may help you to find new ways to do so.

CHAPTER

II

ABOUT GOOD TEACHING

No matter what we have or have not in the way of time, space, and equipment, before beginning to consider what can be done to improve the situation it may be well to remind ourselves of a few important points about good teaching.

1. LEARNING MUST <u>INCLUDE</u> DOING

Because boys and girls, men and women, are the same on Sunday as on any other day, the way they learn in church school will be no different from the way they learn at other times and places. "Children become what they experience." "We learn what we live." "They learn by doing." "We remember 10 per cent of what we hear, 50 per cent of what we see, and 90 per cent of what we do." These and similar phrases are repeated constantly in regard to education. When applied to the church school, they mean that here too learning is best accomplished through firsthand experience.

This is true even of Bible content. Turning often to certain books, stories, passages is a better way to learn what is in the Bible than is merely memorizing references or the names of its books. The life of Jesus, or of any other Biblical character, becomes real as we reproduce Bible lands and times and people by dramatization and research, by making models and maps, as well as by hearing the Bible stories.

But the principle of learning by doing becomes even more important as we teach Christian concepts.

Ted will learn more quickly the meaning of "Serve one another in love" (Gal. 5:13, Moffatt) by sharing the new red truck with Jimmy, who is a visitor today.

Small Susan, whose father died in Korea, shares in a "family" grace at the table in the housekeeping corner, and learns to thank God for everyday blessings.

Carlos has heard his teacher say, "God has planned for all we want and need," and has learned, "The earth is the Lord's and the fulness thereof" (Ps. 24:1). But the words become more meaningful as he discovers one of the wonders of seed distribution in a

prickly seed pod on the primary "table of treasures, " or is reminded
of the dependable regularity of the seasons by a series of pictures
he has been asked to arrange.

Jack and Bob, junior highs, plan and work together as they make
puzzles for the children's ward at the hospital. They learn, too,
to enter into the problems of other people as they choose the right
pictures, the right weight and size for mountings for puzzles that
will be used by bedfast children.

The half dozen families who work in the churchyard on cleanup
day learn many things--the fun of family sharing, the way shared
activity helps in making friends, a pride in "our church."

The principle of learning by doing is important no matter who
is doing the learning--children, young people, or adults--and no
matter what is being learned. We learn best and most that with
which we are actively engaged.

Nursery-kindergarten area, arranged with equipment as listed on
page 9, and as indicated in room diagram, page 11.

2. EACH INDIVIDUAL IS DIFFERENT

Individual differences are important because learning depends
so largely upon what we are interested in, how we feel about
things, what we have previously learned and done.

What we like affects our learning--

Five-year-old Carol likes to explore, to touch, to play
with others.

Primary area, arranged with equipment as listed on page 9, and as indicated in room diagram, page 11.

Six-year-old Bobby plays well alone, but shuns other children.

Ted is sixteen. He likes to experiment and has a keen ear for scientific facts.

Nancy is nineteen. Logical thinking comes hard for her--but she understands people and gets along well with them.

What we have experienced affects our learning--

Four-year-old Ralph has been frequently ill. He cries easily and finds it difficult to leave his mother even for a short period of time.

Joyce, at thirteen, has lived in eight different cities and has crossed the Atlantic twice. She is an only, and a much-loved, child.

Fred, who is fifteen and the oldest of five children, is used to responsibility. He has lived in only one town and has never been out of it.

The differences in these children will determine to a large extent the way in which they meet new situations, and therefore how and what they learn in the same church groups will be different. There is no such thing as an average child. In a sense, there is no such thing as a group--only a group of individuals. Therefore our teaching must be varied enough to open to each pupil (at least sometimes) his roads to learning; to give him opportunities to contribute from his knowledge and experience.

3. DIFFERING INDIVIDUALS CAN BE TAUGHT
IN THE SAME GROUP

This is the difficult task every teacher faces. It is hard to know very much about those you see for only an hour on Sunday morning, and perhaps never see at any other time, although every effort should be made to extend that knowledge in their homes, schools, and so on. But if you cannot see them at other times and places, it is at least true that the more you see them in action--thinking, speaking, working, not just listening--the more you will know of them.

And what you learn must be used, not just noticed or put in a notebook. To try to provide the best possible learning experience for each child is a sound religious concept. Jesus stressed the importance of one sheep, of one coin. He gave time, over and over, to individuals--to Mary of Bethany, Nicodemus, the woman of Samaria, those within his chosen band of apostles. Each was valued for what he was; each found his need met.

You teach many individuals at once, whether they are children, young people, or adults, by providing a wide choice of activities suitable for that general age group. You use, not one approach or method, but many. Each member of the group must have his chance to give and to take, to teach and to learn, in the way most effective for him. To sit still for long periods is real torture for an active body and to do so prevents learning. Some boys and girls are slow readers, poor memorizers (indeed, so are some adults!). To limit your teaching to lectures, turnabout reading, and memory drill will simply mean that some of the group learn not at all.

The teacher must never be merely "a relater of facts"(sometimes facts already known!), "a moralizer," "a keeper of order," "a dispenser of materials." He must be free and able to share the experiences of the group, to guide their thinking and doing, to help individuals grow. In all good teaching the teacher is, of course, the key. Wherever there is a teacher who himself has a real knowledge of Christ, a warm, intelligent love for each pupil, and a winsomeness in his use of good methods for the age he is teaching, good teaching will take place.

Two views of the junior area, arranged with equipment as listed on page 9, and as indicated in room diagram, page 11.

CHAPTER

III

FACING YOUR PROBLEMS

It takes real teaching genius and equally real consecration to triumph over the limitations of time, space, and equipment with which most of us have to struggle in church schools. Our task is much harder, whether we teach nursery children or adults, if we have to contend constantly with distraction, noise, disorder, overcrowding, and an almost complete lack of helpful tools.

It is generally agreed that in the usual one-hour session of church school forty minutes should be set aside for class or group teaching, as over against worship or other "general assembly" purposes. If your teachers are giving their work proper preparation, they need that much time. Do they have it? If not, you might ask a few questions and perhaps find ways to:

SAVE TIME

Is it necessary to have both opening and closing "exercises"? Remember, moving from place to place takes time!

Is time wasted waiting for something to happen? Could not pupils go directly to class upon arrival, finding their teacher there, with something worth-while for the first arrival to do?

Are warning bells really necessary? They mean five minutes
of lost attention! Of course, if there is worship at the close of
the session, there can be a musical signal to call the group together. But teachers should be watching the time anyhow--so
why not let them?

AVOID INTERRUPTIONS

Are you losing time by permitting constant interruptions? Is
it not possible that:

a. Supplies and record books can be put at the meeting places
of all groups before the session begins?

b. A rule can be made--and observed!--that no one interrupt
a class or department session except for a real emergency? Very
Important Persons, including parents, superintendent, and minister,
should save visitors, friendly expressions of interest, and questions or announcements for some other time--except by special
and advance arrangement with those concerned.

c. The offering be made a part of worship? Or the offering
and class record be turned in to the secretary and treasurer at
the end of the session, with the report given or posted the following
week?

The types of interruption indicated here are very real obstacles
to good teaching. Every minute saved is a help. Many of them can
be gained if your church school staff face such questions as these
together. Any changes made should be voted upon by the proper
bodies, and explained to all concerned before being put into oper-
ation.

REDUCE NOISE

Noise is a consumer of both time and space--causing inatten-
tion, and making the space we have seem smaller. It is well for
all teachers to know that a voice low in volume and pitch holds
attention better, is heard more easily, is less apt to carry to
other groups, and will be imitated by all! Noise can sometimes
be reduced by placing a teacher in the center rather than at the
edge of a group, or by arranging a class so that its members talk
toward a wall rather than toward another class.

Even such apparently minor matters as floor coverings, rubber
heels, and care in handling chairs and closing doors enter into
this problem of noise. Using a plan worked out by two of the boys,
one group of juniors actually practiced moving their chairs from a
worship situation into adjoining class circles without the usual
duel of chair legs that had been producing bedlam. This kind of
thing can be done with humor, facing a common problem, and
making a challenge of its solution. Of course, reminders are
necessary from time to time!

Let us learn, however, to distinguish between noise that can
be avoided and the hum and buzz of interested activity, which dis-
turbs no one who is equally interested!

19

CLEAR OUT WHAT IS NOT NEEDED

Perhaps, even after taking care of all the above matters of organization you still have space problems. It is, of course, possible that your situation can be improved without adding anything at all. The liberal use of dustcloths and mops, the cleaning of closets and straightening of materials on shelves--yes, even unloading the top of the piano--would at least show that someone cares about the atmosphere of a room in which boys and girls, men and women, are guided in the worship of God and the study of his Word! Mending broken chairs and tables; discarding unneeded furniture; disposing of or using leftover materials; washing or dyeing dirty or faded curtains; giving walls or furniture a coat of fresh, light-toned paint--any or all of these will make teaching situations both more spacious and more attractive. Do not leave such matters entirely to the sexton, be he volunteer, part time or full time. He usually has more than enough to do.

Much can be gained in the way of space by taking a good look at your furniture and equipment--both what it is and where it is. The next two chapters will guide you in thinking about this matter. But meanwhile consider whether a large heavy table is needed, if it prevents the primary class from trying dramatization, or other "moving about" activities. Can worktables be hinged to a wall? Would good floor coverings make a space available for young children which is natural to them? And there are many kinds of space-saver equipment listed and described on the latter pages of this book (see Chapters VI , VII, IX). If space is limited, every piece of furniture or equipment must be justified, possibly on several counts; must really be needed and constantly used.

GET WHAT IS NEEDED

In the next two brief sections of this book an attempt is made to list and explain the need for certain basic furnishings and equipment. They are the ones generally agreed to be important for good teaching of the kind we are considering. As you study them, try to avoid thinking, "Oh, I can't do that!"--but rather, "What have we (or what can we get or make) that can be adapted for such use?" But also consider: "Do we understand clearly the teaching purposes to which this equipment can be put? If not, how can we learn to use it effectively?" The answers to these latter questions should be found in the teaching guides you are using from week to week. If they are not, perhaps some questions should be asked in that connection also!

So here is where you begin--by a clear analysis of what you have in the way of time, space, and equipment, and a consideration of what can be done to improve matters. Whatever you decide to adapt, make, or otherwise provide, be sure that all decisions and plans are made by common agreement of those concerned or affected and that proper official action is taken when needed. Be

20

sure also that you do not settle for a makeshift job; the results of your work must be good--well-made, well-placed, sturdy, attractive. Nor do you want to lose sight of the possibility of having sometime a really adequate building for Christian education. Here, we have some first, easy steps in a process that never ends--making what is good, better!

Putting away lapboards, such as are described on page 53.

CHAPTER

IV

THE RIGHT GENERAL EQUIPMENT

For groups above the preschool (primary through adults) the problems concerning equipment are very much the same, differing in amount, size, and the use made of it. For instance, since primary children in general cannot read well, shelves for hymnals and Bibles are of little importance; but clear lettering of the Scripture, poems, or songs they are to learn--in the script used in the local schools and on a surface large enough to be seen by all--becomes quite necessary. The primary department does need shelves for a wide variety of materials, however; and the writing surface for the primary group, whether it be a blackboard or a paper chart, is useful in older groups for recording points of discussion, displaying maps, and so on.

Let us never accept what is the only too common conclusion--that variety in teaching (and hence the need for equipment) concerns only those who teach children. The dull sameness of the teaching of young people and adults has much to do with the progressive rate of loss to the church school in these groups. Therefore, all the furnishings and equipment mentioned here have to do with all age groups, differing only in the use made of them. In general, these are the necessary items (see Chapter VIII for detailed descriptions):

1. A place for wraps. Removing hats, coats, and gloves (especially those of children and their teachers) not only makes for comfort in a stuffy room but takes away that "let's get this over and go" look so evident in church groups.

2. Seating, such as chairs, benches, stools, pews. If possible, these should be the proper height for each age group (see page 47). Plan your seating arrangements so that pupils can see each other as well as the teacher.

3. Tables, as needed for writing and other work activities. For proper heights, see page 47. Rectangular tables waste less space than round ones. For many ways of meeting this need, see pages 52, 53. This is not a constant need, so a place to put tables when not needed is a problem to be faced.

4. Storage space, for supplies. Books, Bibles, hymnals, extra printed materials, paper, pencils, maps, charts, equipment to use in worship--all these are constant needs. There can be a general supply closet or cabinet, with a competent person in charge of it; or such space can be provided for each group (see pages 54-57).

5. Partitions. In a room that must be shared by several classes or age groups some type of movable partition may be a great help in reducing noise and confusion (see pages 58-62).

6. Display surfaces, to use before a group, such as blackboards and bulletin boards. These can be movable, and used to display pictures, maps, charts, or for written records. Easels of various types can be used for some of the same purposes (see pages 62-69).

7. Display space for books and pamphlets. We want to keep informed and to think together about our concerns as Christians, and must therefore make good Christian literature readily available to all (see pages 66-67).

8. A picture file. Good pictures, carefully mounted and filed in such a way as to make them readily available, are an asset in any teaching situation (see pages 70, 71). Maps and charts can be similarly filed for general use.

9. Church school records and the necessary equipment for keeping them carefully (see page 72).

10. Worship equipment (see page 73). In regard to this matter, equipment can be very simple. Since the center of Protestant worship is God rather than a place or objects, our needs at this point are, in the main, a Bible, good hymnals, and offering plates. Of course we will see that the place in which we worship is clean, orderly, and as beautiful as we can make it. This is our service toward God, however, and not a matter of inducing a mood. If we teach our children the real meaning of worship and arrange worship services with all those present in mind, young as well as old; if we plan each service carefully, never making a last minute choice of Scripture, of hymns and a person to play them, of someone to lead in prayer; if we give those present an opportunity to participate rather than merely to listen, we will together come to know and feel the real meaning of group worship--"the worshiping congregation"--in our church school sessions and homes, as well as in the regular worship of the church service.

Two additional suggestions concerning the place of worship should be mentioned, however. When it is necessary to meet in a room completely lacking in any worship elements, and full of somewhat distracting furnishings (as in a kitchen), it is well to plan a background of some kind for the side of the room toward which the children face--a large screen, a triptych(see page 73), hangings of some plain, deep color. This need be only wide and high enough to form a place to focus attention.

It is well, in children's groups, to make the arrangement of the place of worship each Sunday morning one of the services the children perform. Therefore, instead of some fixed setting or equipment, there could be shared planning, by teacher and several children, of a way to express what together they will be thinking about in worship. This might be done by flowers, a picture on an easel, a globe, a Bible. For primary groups the arrangement might include a bulletin board or turnover chart on which words of Scripture or hymns to be read or sung together have been lettered. At times the arrangement might be related to gifts which are to be dedicated, or to faraway friends for whom they are praying, and so on. In older groups such preparation would include the placing of hymnals and Bibles where they will be needed, and in careful advance preparation for each detail of the service.

For suggested room arrangements of the equipment listed above in various types of situations and for various age groups above the preschool, see pages 11, 32, 33, 37. For ways of adapting or increasing the space available, or for making better use of it, see Chapter VI.

Spatter-painted hangings make effective room decorations.

V

THE RIGHT EQUIPMENT FOR YOUNG CHILDREN

It is possible to create a good environment for young children in any church building--a place where each child is interested and happy, confident that the church is a place where he is loved and where his needs will be met. Fortunately, for both nursery and kindergarten children (and they should be separated if at all possible), space is more important than furnishings. The floor is the natural habitat of young children, and tables and chairs can be dispensed with,in favor of a good and cleanable floor covering. The teacher who attempts to keep little children seated around a bare table, or in the same chairs on the same spot for an hour on Sunday morning, is apt to complain of disinterest and discipline problems. (See Chapter II.)

Young children, when interested in what they are doing, are little disturbed either by sight or sound, particularly the latter. But so they may have freedom of movement without disturbing others, it is perhaps wise to give them space that can be screened off, even if this means some limitation as to its size. On the other hand, by the very nature of the child, this is the group that most needs space. Therefore we will not continue to be satisfied with a small corner if there is any possibility of extending the available space in any of the ways suggested in Chapter VI.

For both nursery and kindergarten we should work toward enough room to:

> permit the arrangement of a wide variety of materials and equipment in work-and-play centers in which the child is free to make choices.

> provide opportunities for the child to play in small groups of his own choosing, or alone, if he so desires.

> give the teacher opportunity to guide those who most need her, while others are safely, happily, and constructively occupied.

All this is especially important, since there are many occasions other than Sunday morning at the church school hour at which preschool children may be in the church building. There may be care groups for them during weekday meetings for adults; there is a growing need for weekday play groups and for well-established weekday nursery schools and kindergartens under church auspices; there are care groups in many churches that extend through the morning church service. All these call for a more relaxed and varied program, and therefore more and better equipment.

Several basic work-and-play centers have special value for Christian education and are also a natural part of the child's limited world. Each of them can be very simple or quite elaborate. They can all be available every Sunday or, where space is at a premium, one or more of them can be set up for use only on days when they contribute most to the teaching purpose. They are:

1. FOR BROWSING

Books and pictures are of first importance; but also such things as a "Bible times" house, tent, or scroll (perhaps made and presented by a group of older children); simple costumes, the right size to wear; puzzles and toys to pull or manipulate; a record player, carefully chosen records, and rhythm instruments; objects connected with nature, such as magnets, plants, an aquarium, a magnifying glass, and treasures from outdoors--for a child to see, hear, talk about, and use.

2. FOR FAMILY PLAY

This is vital, since the young child's whole existence centers in the home and his main occupation is "playing" what he sees the adults there do. The care of the young and weak, consideration for older people, family tasks by which we "serve one another in love" (Gal. 5:13, Moffatt), times of prayer at table and bedside, all become a part of this teaching play. If possible, the equipment here should be large enough for <u>real</u> use; if not, children love "little things." Usable items, somewhat in the order of their importance, are:

dolls	extra doll clothes
a doll bed	bedding
kitchen equipment	laundry equipment
tea table	dishes
a toy telephone	clothes for "dressing up"

equipment for cleaning up

3. FOR BLOCK PLAY

Make the blocks large enough to really do something with! (See page 84.) Add small stand-up figures (families, community helpers) such as are provided in the activity packets of most teaching materials; and also pull toys, such as trains and trucks. They will add meaning to the already valuable block play, which gives opportunity for building Christian concepts (ideas) along with the construction of homes, stores, and churches; and also for adventures in co-operation.

4. FOR MAKING THINGS

As in the first section above, this calls for floor or table work space, together with clay, paint, crayons, scissors, paper, and paste. Ways to keep clean and to clean up become important also!

Such centers for work and play are not just a matter of putting out materials--although that should be carefully done, well in advance of the arrival of the first child, or with that child's help. Each object must be thoughtfully chosen and placed in such a way as really to contribute to the child's growth in understanding, co-operation, and skills. For instance, on a Sunday when the idea of "our church" is uppermost, a picture of a family going to church hung in the housekeeping corner and some special doll clothes suggest "getting the children ready for church." In the block corner, another

picture hints at building a church. Near the nature objects, some
flowers and a vase suggest "putting flowers in a vase for our church."
Books and pictures on the browsing table are along the same line;
and an "excursion" around the building can be planned--all adding
to the developing thought. In similar ways Biblical words can be
brought to life--a Bible story, by putting swaddling clothes on a
doll, arranging creche figures, or "posing" a much-loved Nativity
picture; a verse or verses by putting into practice, "Serve one
another in love" (Gal. 5:13, Moffatt; see page 13 also), or by learning
better to understand, "God giveth us . . . all things to enjoy" (I Tim.
6:17, K.J.V.).

By thoughtful adaptation such activities as these can be carried
on, if necessary, in the small corner in front of or behind your
pews; or can be extended as much as time and space permit. Guidance in their detailed use in a planned program cannot be given here,
but is given in the lesson plans of good denominational teaching
guides.

On the pages indicated you will find suggested arrangements of
such equipment for:

CHAPTER

VI

ADAPTING THE SPACE YOU HAVE

By now some of you may be thinking: That's all very well--we know we could arrange what we have better, and we know there are many things we need. But ours is a peculiar situation!

Of course it is. Each of us faces different problems, although some of them are remarkably similar. That is just why no book can give you final answers--it can only be a helpful guide toward finding some for yourself. But realizing the limitations of those of us who tried to work out the first experiment at West Maryville, and how we had to fumble along toward our solutions, we are convinced that any group of people who really want to do so can solve their space problems--or at least improve their setup. From what we hear, space troubles are largely of three types:

The Problem of Too Little Space. This would include the one-room church as well as many others that do not have enough rooms or enough room within the rooms!

The Problem of Large, Echoing Empty Space (such as fellowship halls and gymnasiums) that must be shared with others or reduced to livable proportions.

The Problem of Space That Is Yours Only on Sunday Morning-- rooms in the church which are also used for other purposes; or "borrowed" space in a schoolhouse or grange hall, or even in a private home.

Read again Chapter III, which is a guide for the analysis of your troubles about space. Then here are some suggestions that may help you.

1. TOO LITTLE SPACE

Would it be well to regroup or rearrange the use of the space you have? (For instance, as at West Maryville, arranging the youth group in a more compact way. Compare pages 10 and 11.)

Do some groups now occupy a larger space than they need, while others are crowded? It might be well to consider the size of each group and its average attendance in relation to the spaces available. "The greatest good for the greatest number" must be a guiding principle in a Christian church as well as in democratic government!

Is there space somewhere that you have not thought of using--a hallway that can be kept clear of traffic, a storeroom, a corner of the kitchen, a balcony, the space back of the last pews?

If you have exhausted all possibilities in the church itself, is there available space nearby--in a home (not the manse!), a store, the grange hall, a school building? In one small village the church "lends" its preschool rooms to the public school for use during the week in return for the use of some of the schoolrooms on Sunday, for older groups.

Is it possible to plan a schedule that allows for double use of at least some of your space? Some churches across the country are having double and triple sessions of both the Sunday morning worship service and church school. But where two or more services of worship are not needed there are ways to double up the teaching sessions by having more than one session of church school; or by having certain groups of younger children (probably preschool) held during the church service; or by having some youth or adult groups meet for study at some other time--Sunday evening, or even during the week.

If you are in a favorable climate, have you made full use of the outdoors? One church divided an old carriage shed into usable sections!

Some Answers to the Above Questions
a. Use of Pews in a One-Room Church

It is important, as has been said, that pupils see each other as well as the teacher, if there is to be good discussion and other types of participation. By unscrewing several front or back pews from the floor, and assigning the job of placing and replacing them each Sunday morning to a class of men or older boys, some effective arrangements such as the three given here can be managed. If desired, movable screens (see page 58) can be put between or behind them, although this is not necessary if the group face a wall and keep their voices low. A box for supplies for each class stained to match the pew finish can be stored under one of the pews. Folding tables of several types could be used in such groupings if needed.

This arrangement is probably the easiest because it is made by simply turning one pew around to face the other. Here too, pupils are able to see each other during discussions.

The U arrangement could be made along any wall. Here too, the pupils face the wall and each other and are not distracted by other groups.

This figure shows the type of arrangement possible in a corner. The pupils are facing the wall, and there is room for movement.

b. Use of the Outdoors

Many churches are in a beautiful natural setting that could be improved and made more useful with just a little thought and work. If there is a grove of trees, the underbrush could be cleared out, and grass and shrubs planted around the church. If there is an open lawn, arbors, covered with vines for shade, might be the answer. Church and community groups often work together to build picnic tables and fireplaces. The former could be just as useful on Sunday as throughout the week, if they are placed and spaced in such a way as to make them available to groups of children or young people on Sunday mornings or for vacation church school.

Even without such construction, classes could meet outdoors whenever possible, using folding chairs or benches. Cement blocks with

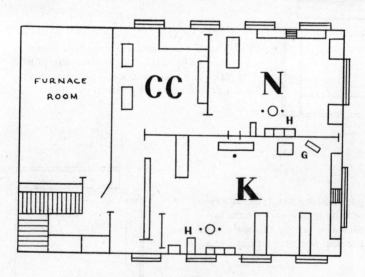

Basement room planned for preschool groups. For key see page 42.

32

boards placed across have been used in such situations for seating
and for worktable space. Other types of permanent outdoor equipment can be made with rocks or adobe. For younger children, chairs
are not needed, for they can sit comfortably on the grass, or on a
blanket or two kept at the church for that purpose. Just as each
class in the small church might have a box of supplies under a
pew, just so such a box can be carried into the churchyard, if the
group is meeting there.

Churches in areas in which the winter weather is not so balmy
may nevertheless make good use of outdoor space during the summer.

c. The Two-Room Church

Often a church building has just one room other than the sanctu-
ary--a full basement. If so, it is well to use it for the younger
children, as they need more space per person than any other group.
Also, it is wise to separate, for all or most of the session, the
primary from the preschool children, even though there are only
a few of each. The first diagram below gives a possible arrangement for such a room for the preschool children only; the second,
for its use by preschool, primary, and junior groups. This is a
good division, since these younger children all need their own
special kinds of experience in church school. Notice that the room
is not cut up with permanent partitions, for in the small church
it probably has many other uses. For types of movable partitions,
see pages 58-63. If necessary, the juniors fit more readily with
young people and adults.

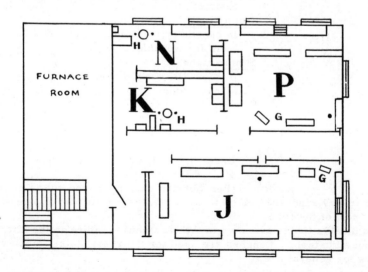

Basement room planned for all children's groups. For key see
page 42.

d. Multiple Sessions

More and more churches are finding multiple sessions the only solution to their problems--and a most practical one. Some new churches are actually planning to use their facilities this way, rather than to build huge plants which are in the main occupied only on Sunday mornings, for one session. Because this is a comparatively new trend, we're giving in detail the way in which two churches have planned for two or more sessions of their church schools, one small (150 members) and the other larger (300).

To do this, a church must study carefully its own situation rather than take over another plan throughout. Much depends on the distances families must come; whether neighborhood car pools are possible; whether a number of families live within walking distance; what the local Sunday habits are. Even more depends upon getting a wholehearted response to the plan on the part of the congregation-- at least a willingness to try it! One thing is sure: enrollment of a child must be for a particular session--there can be no changing back and forth from week to week.

Example I
Schedule:

9:00-9:50 A.M.	Primary department: Rooms I, II, III (in basement); largest department--average attendance 60; 6 classes
10:00-10:50 A.M.	Juniors: Rooms I, II Junior highs: In sanctuary; seniors joined them for worship Senior highs: In room III, spilled over to furnace room! Adults: In pastor's study
11:00-12:00 A.M.	Nursery and kindergarten: (In basement during church service) Under 3, in kitchen; 3's, in room II 4's and 5's, in room I (Benches and chairs cleared out as needed)

The nursery-kindergarten staff is double, to permit church attendance half of the time.

Adjustable tables are used in the basement. Tables in the kitchen are not adjustable. Benches are used for the short tables; tubular chairs for general use.

Portable screens divide the classes. They are numbered to go in same places each week, so class work need not be removed. One large bulletin board is shared by the various superintendents using

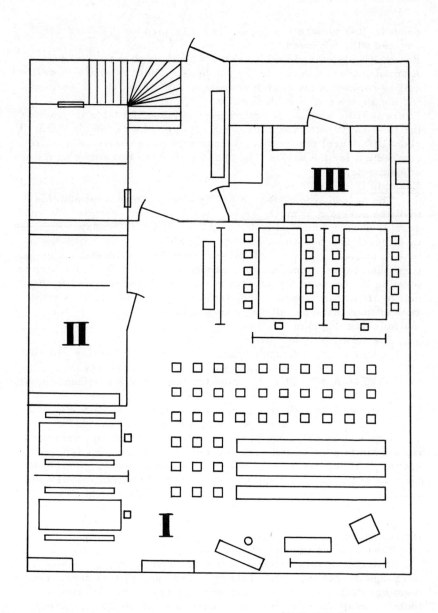

III

II

I

926080

35

room I. The picture file cabinet has a lectern top. Tables are covered with velveteen.

Room II is also the church library, with shelves to the ceiling. A small ladder is available for use here. There is also a floor-to-ceiling cabinet in the church secretary's office which has sections for the supplies of each department.

There is little shifting of equipment. In room II a table is used for the first shift; just chairs for the second; no chairs for the third. In room III(kitchen) the first and second shifts use chairs, which are cleared out for the babies. Boys and girls take turns making these adjustments.

Example II

The second type of church having a well-thought-out plan for multiple sessions is much larger, having a membership of 480 and regular church school attendance of over 300 each Sunday. Although this church now has a new educational unit, it was built with the intention of continuing the multiple-session plan. With this congregation, the concern is not only for economical use of space but also for meeting the needs of the parents of young children who find it difficult to attend, in sequence, both church school and church worship. Both of these have definitely increased in attendance under the multiple-session plan.

The schedule is as follows:

9:00 A.M. Church school for all ages, beginning with two-and-a-half-year-olds in the nursery.

10:00 A.M. Church school for the junior department and below. Church worship, with nursery care.

11:00 A.M. Church school for primary department and below. Church worship, with nursery care.

With occasional unavoidable exceptions, each pupil is enrolled for a definite session and does not move back and forth from one to another. There has been no difficulty in getting teaching personnel because of the increased number of interested parents. Those without training or experience are asked to sit in the department as an observer before undertaking any part in the work. Families are encouraged to consider the whole situation before choosing the hour for attendance or for accepting staff responsibility.

The following information may be helpful:

"There is a superintendent for each department, and also a leader in charge of each session. This calls for well-planned departmental meetings each quarter and sometimes oftener. The superintendent looks in on all the sessions and usually is available to help when needed. The leader for each session is responsible for worship plans, and in general acts as a superintendent, but for only that one hour."

Obviously, there can and must be endless variations to these two plans, based on local needs. But they indicate the creative and thoughtful way individual churches are facing problems of space.

2. TOO MUCH SPACE

If your church has a fellowship hall, gymnasium, or some other room for large gatherings, you probably have the problem of its use on Sunday mornings by several small groups. The diagram on page 33 gives a possible use of a basement by preschool, primary, and junior groups.

It is a real accomplishment to make usable units of space in a large room where nothing of a permanent nature can be left in place, or where there is the problem of several groups meeting at one time. Review the procedure of the one-room church in Chapter I, for the problems are similar.

If by chance this large room must be used by one small group, do not spread out all over it, but use screens, curtains, or some other device to shut off the part you really need. Too much space is an invitation to disorder and disunity.

Here are a few suggested aids to such an effort:

1. Good screens that will reduce both sound and sight between groups. These screens may double as bulletin boards, wrap racks, or supply cabinets, depending upon your particular need. (See pages 58-62).

2. Portable supply cupboards for each class. The one shown on page 55 was made to fit with several others to form the serving space when the kitchen was in use during the week. Supplies could be kept in them permanently.

3. Portable tables for use in the dining room (seating 8 to 10) with legs adjustable to different heights. Dining tables could then be used for various age groups on Sunday.

The diagram below shows the setup of a large basement room for a primary or junior department. This type of arrangement is recommended rather than having a room for worship and little "cubicles" for each class. A much freer use of the space is possible, and the room can be used for other groups as well.

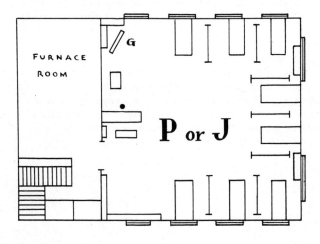

FURNACE ROOM

G

P or J

Basement room for a large primary or junior group. For key see page 42.

3. SHARED SPACE

The problem of space shared by groups meeting at different times is twofold--for the church that uses its rooms for many different activities during the week, and for the church that meets in a building which it borrows just on Sundays. In both, the basic problem is storage of equipment. This problem is an acute one in any church, for few churches were originally built with places to store the amount of equipment needed by the various groups used by the churches of today.

Sharing a Room at Different Hours

One suggestion is that a storage closet might be built along an entire wall of a room used by several groups, with compartments for the particular furniture and supplies used by each. Such a cabinet could be made an attractive part of the room. Each section should be neatly kept by its owners, and the rights of ownership should be strictly observed! See pages 54 ff. Note also the suggestions in the previous section, "Too Much Space," page 37.

Central Storage Closet

Another suggestion is that of a central storage closet for supplies. Here is how one church found this a real solution to its problems:

A former primary superintendent, who wanted a change of church school work and saw the great need for proper care of supplies, worked with the teachers of the church school to clear out a small room that was cluttered with odds and ends. Some shelves were built, and a table was repaired and placed in the room. The "keeper of supplies" is on hand early every Sunday morning. She not only keeps everything clean and in order but helps to secure supplies as they are needed. Supplies include vases, easels, teaching pictures, song charts, work materials such as construction paper, oak tag, pencils, crayons, paste. Lesson materials and books are kept here also as they come in. This keeper of supplies has a group of people on the lookout for pictures from all sources which might be helpful to teachers. These she labels, mounts, and files. She makes many of the song charts, posters, or printed cards for memory work that are needed. She meets with teachers to help them list supplies needed for a coming quarter's work, and sees that such supplies are available. This storage room has eliminated several untidy, disorderly cupboards which took up unnecessary space, besides keeping the materials in better condition and making them available to more than one department at a time. It has also proved to be a morale booster for the teachers in knowing that someone is willing to help them secure needed supplies.

If at all possible, try to have the young children meet in rooms that are not used for adult groups during the week. There is so much equipment for them that storage presents a real problem. Often their room can be used for care groups during the week, while adult meetings are being held. More and more churches are also having weekday nursery schools or kindergartens when they have adequate facilities and leadership.

Use of a Kitchen

For groups, such as juniors, that need working surfaces for projects, the kitchen can be a good place in which to meet. And if the boys and girls are kept interested, they'll take pride in not meddling with items in the kitchen that are not for their use.

Screens or hangings can be made (see page 58) to cut off the view of part of the kitchen equipment. These screens can be used for bulletin boards and writing space for the teacher also.

Certain equipment for the kitchen might be made with the classes that meet there in mind. A working surface, for instance, can be hinged to fold up against the wall, having a bulletin board underneath. Supply cabinets (see page 54) can be made to fit under working surfaces and so be out of sight when not in use.

Use of Other Buildings

There are also problems to face if you meet in a building which you borrow just on Sunday. This is the common plight of many of our finest, fastest growing church schools, for almost each new church being formed has to meet almost anywhere before finally having its own building. And older churches face this problem when forced to hold classes in nearby homes or stores until more building space can be found--or when a fire means there is no building at all!

Because so many groups are able to use schoolrooms special attention is first given to this situation.

Meeting in a schoolhouse may have some real advantages--although at best it is usually a temporary arrangement. If the school is a large one and well furnished, there is the advantage of having equipment of the proper size for various ages. If details are worked out in a friendly way with the public-school teachers, often such furnishings may be used, but never, of course, the regular supplies. The P. T. A. and the church school may even co-operate in the purchase of equipment to be used by both groups.

If no closet space is available in the school building, a separate cabinet can be made or bought to hold church school supplies, in order to avoid toting. Such a cabinet should be locked.

4. TOTING SUPPLIES

When it comes to teaching aids the church school teacher has a triple problem: church storage, home storage, and weekly transportation. If the latter two are the problem--as they are when rooms are shared--it is an advantage if a combined solution can be found. This calls for lightweight containers that can be carried easily from place to place and do not take up too much room.

The first one is made from a square or round hatbox, or from a small packing box, and is a carrier for three-dimensional objects, such as dioramas, models, etc. Often they can be planned to form their own container. For instance, if the top and one side of a box are removed to make a stage for a puppet show or diorama, keep them; hinge the side to the top with gummed paper, and when the scene is not in use it can be enclosed for protection. Such objects can also be kept in large paper or cellophane bags, labeled, and hung like bird cages from the rafters or from a pole such as is used for coat hangers. Add a sturdy handle of cloth or tape.

The second is a carrier for flat pictures (mounted or unmounted), maps, charts, and so on that must be kept flat. It is made from two large sheets of corrugated cardboard, held together and carried by cotton tape put on with rivets or long paper fasteners. Materials of this same kind that can be rolled may be put in tubes cut from one of the large kind used to deliver rugs or linoleum, riveting in a handle (such handles can be held by knots as well as rivets) of tape or of heavy paper rope or cord.

The fourth is a carryall made from any sturdy cardboard carton--

a real basket can of course be used if you have a good one. Cardboard divisions fitted into this (or marked boxes, cellophane or glass containers) will keep smaller articles from getting mixed or lost. Carrying handles of the kinds mentioned can be added. Some teachers have used an inexpensive shoebag (the kind with pockets) to hold supplies, rolling it to carry home in such a container, and hanging it within reach in any available place--even on the back of a pew--each Sunday. Illustrative materials, such as small pictures, can be kept in Manila folders or in a file from the ten-cent store.

The key words for such toting equipment should be:

1. Lightweight--and no excessive bulk.

2. Durable--for instance, reinforce the holes through which handles are put by rivets, or by patches of cloth or tape.

3. Orderly--keep the various kinds of things tidily arranged and separate.

4. Attractive--paint or stain or cover in some way containers that are unsightly. They can even be decorated with wallpaper cutouts, or designs made with crayons or poster paints, and shellacked.

It is possible to buy at Army-Navy surplus stores what is known in the Navy as "tote boxes"--medium-sized, heavy cardboard boxes, with a handhold cut into one end. These are good to use for toting within a building. (See also, "For Traveling Teachers," page 92.)

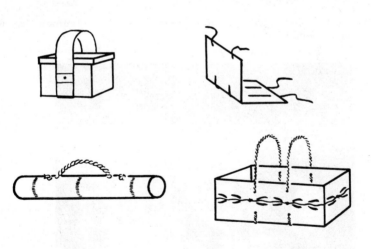

KEY TO ROOM DIAGRAMS

Page 32--A basement room planned for preschool groups:
        CC--Care Center--including cribs, a playpen, a cupboard
        N--Nursery
        K--Kindergarten

Page 33-- A basement room planned for all children's groups:
        N--Nursery
        K--Kindergarten
        P--Primary
        J--Junior

Page 37-- A basement room planned for a large primary or junior group:
        P or J--Primary or Junior

In N and K, page 32, and in K, page 33, H is the housekeeping center, for family play.

In K, page 32, in P and J, page 33, and on page 37, G is for group assembly, and includes a piano, a teacher's table, and a display easel.

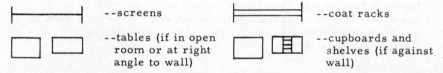

        --screens   --coat racks

        --tables (if in open room or at right angle to wall)   --cupboards and shelves (if against wall)

    Chairs are not included in room diagrams; it is assumed they will be placed as needed.

CHAPTER
VII

SETTING UP A WORKSHOP

Now that you have thought of your own church and its needs in
the light of adaptations that other groups have found successful,
you are ready to begin to carry out your plans. If you've been
doing this dreaming by yourself, now is the time to share it; so
talk it over with other teachers, parents, or church officers. If
any major change is to be made, the best judgement of all those
concerned will be needed. Even if you are just thinking of how
better to arrange your own classroom, let others share your plans.
Parents are usually eager to assist in anything that will help their
own children. Try to find at least one other person to work with
you--but proceed on your own if necessary.

Look carefully at the suggestions for actual equipment in the
next chapter. Before making equipment, plan for its use and for
storage when not in use.

Don't overlook possibilities of using pieces of furniture that are
already made. Bureaus, tables, bookshelves, and other pieces
of furniture that might be useful in the church school can frequently
be found around the church building and in the attics of church
members. Auction and secondhand stores often have sturdy furniture at great reductions. But do not accept or buy such furniture
unless you are sure it can be effectively used, and can be repaired
or refinished if necessary to look well in its surroundings.

Now you are ready for specific planning. It is quite possible to
change a department completely at no expense whatever! After the
equipment that is to be made is decided upon, list the supplies necessary to make it. Most of them can be obtained at little expense.
Enlist the co-operation of local merchants. While types of materials
will vary in different parts of the country, it is possible everywhere
to find what is called for, or an acceptable substitute. Make copies
of the list of supplies and distribute them to parents and various
church groups with an explanation of the project.

BY WHOM SHALL THE WORK BE DONE?

Those who have helped you in the planning will probably be

happy to help in the construction. You could, of course, do it by yourself, or you might be able to have it done by a professional, if money is no object. Even then you would miss the fellowship that comes when dads, grandmothers, and friends work together. Their attitude toward the church school will never be the same after the thrill of producing some needed equipment. So look around the congregation for those who would love to work on such a project: older men and women who need to be needed, men who would hesitate to speak in a meeting but could surely speak with their hands, older boys and girls who want "something to do, " young people's groups feeling the thrill of a call to service.

It is surely true that men and women of no previous experience can make very satisfactory equipment, and will love doing so. And there is a warm feeling of pride in being able to say, "I helped make that!"

WHERE CAN THE WORK BE DONE?

Probably most of the work will be done in the church itself--in the basement, or in the room for which the equipment is intended. There are churches that have old tables on hand for such "workings, " which may also be used by the vacation church school for craftwork and even as "extras" for church suppers. Boards put across chairs, sawhorses, or wooden boxes make fairly good working surfaces. Using good church tables may be tempting, but it is bad for public relations!

There may be in the home of one of the church members a workshop with space enough so that several interested people can work at once under the direction of a "do it yourself" enthusiast.

A church that has room and enough projects upon which to work might well set up a permanent workshop to be used by hobby groups as well as by groups interested in doing things for the church. Some churches have saved real sums of money in repairs and new equipment in this way, and have at the same time provided an opportunity for many to serve the church.

PLANNING A WORK SESSION

Where only two or three people work together, organization of the job is not the main point, although space, supplies, and tools are necessary. However, if you are planning a work night for a larger group, these directions and cautions may prove helpful:

1. All plans for needed equipment should have been carefully made ahead of time.
2. All necessary supplies and all tools should be on hand.
3. Directions for each project should be written out and placed by the materials needed for it.
4. There should be at least one person who knows the details of each project available as consultant, moving about to see the progress each group is making.

NECESSARY TOOLS

Tools should be placed in some order, either in a toolbox, on a supply board, or on a table. The place for each should be labeled so that it can be returned after use. Each borrowed tool should be labeled--possibly by writing the name on adhesive tape and sticking it on the tool. It is best for the workers to bring as many of the tools as possible to avoid responsibility for borrowed tools.

Tools for a Work Group of Ten to Fifteen:

2 saws--the ordinary hand crosscut variety
1 keyhole saw for any sawing in tight places
1 coping saw for cutting curves
4 hammers, at least two of which should have heads with which nails can be taken out (claw hammers). The rest can be anything to pound with
2 screw drivers
2 pairs of pliers
1 pair of tin snips
3 yardsticks for measuring and drawing straight lines
1 metal measuring tape will help in measuring greater distances
2 pairs of scissors for general cutting
1 penknife for small cutting and whittling
1 old butcher knife for cutting linoleum, etc.
For cutting cardboard, knives with razor edges are sometimes available
1 plane--to be used by a skilled workman
1 brace and bit--to be used by a skilled workman
1 square for making square corners
1 level for putting up shelves that are level
Pencils and paper for drawing plans
Paintbrushes of assorted sizes
Newspapers--stacks of them--for putting under work, painting, etc.
Glass jars in which to keep nails and small pieces of hardware, so they can be seen easily
Assorted tin cans for cleaning brushes, mixing paint, etc.

Assorted nails, screws, and other hardware needed
Sandpaper, and blocks of wood to put it on
1 wood file for smoothing down very rough wood
If much old lumber is to be torn apart, a smaller wrecking bar
will prove useful
If cutting edges are dull, and there's anyone who knows how to
sharpen them, a carborundum whetstone will save the group
much time
Sticks for stirring paint
Cleanup Materials:
Turpentine or thinner for cleaning brushes
Old rags for cleaning brushes, wiping up paint spots, etc.
Facilities for wash-up--basin, soap, turpentine, towels
Old clothes available to wear during painting or dirty work

TRAINING WORKERS

You will know your own group and just how amateur they are in
this work. If they have never done painting, hammering, or other
such work, it will probably be good to have the group together for
a short period of instruction before putting them to work. This will
save many questions and mistakes.

Give the purpose of each tool, showing where it is placed and
should be returned when not in use. Power tools and others that
might be damaged by wrong use should be handled only under super-
vision.

Give instruction in tearing boxes apart, so as to save both nails
and lumber. If you yourself do not know the "hows," ask someone
who is a carpenter to work with your group. In almost every church
there is at least one capable carpenter who would be glad to help.

It is well to have a simple first-aid kit handy with Band-Aids,
and so on, for cut fingers.

Check on the use of the room in which you expect to work. Sat-
urday night is a poor time for painting church school rooms and
furniture!

Be sure that someone is responsible for cleaning up the room
after the work is over.

Now you are ready to proceed, and may you have as much fun
and real satisfaction as others have had before you!

CONSTRUCTION NOTES

Here are a few helpful hints for construction of the equipment
described in the following chapters. Remember, work on most of
these items has been done by amateurs. An attempt has been made
to make directions understandable to amateurs, and yet as far as
possible to "real" carpenters too.

Sizes

You'll notice that few exact dimensions are given. That's because the boxes and other materials used will vary from place to

place, and we want you to use what is available. Please do not say (as some have said), "We have only apple boxes: we can't use patterns calling for orange crates!" Apple boxes are sturdier anyway! But for your help, here are the dimensions of the three types of boxes most frequently used in the patterns:

apple boxes--19 1/2" x 11" x 12"
orange crates--26" x 12" x 12"
Tokay grape boxes--18" x 14" x 6"
(Other fruit lugs are about this same size)

However, you will want to make the furniture the right size for the children involved.

Here are the heights usually given for furniture for children:

Age	Chairs (seat height)	Table Surfaces	Working Surfaces (as ironing boards)
Nursery (age 3)	8"	18"	about 22"
Kindergarten (age 4, 5)	10"	20"	about 24"
Primary (grades 1, 2, 3)	14"	24"	
Junior (grades 4, 5, 6)	16"	26"	

Dimensions of Tables

For nursery and kindergarten children, a rectangular table 20" x 30" is most usable as a tea table or as a working surface for two children (sitting on opposite sides of the table).

Materials

Chapter X lists materials that can be used and where they can be found. Scrap materials have been used in construction, so that churches having little money can have good equipment. You'll soon learn to keep your eyes open for all the types used, and you'll surely find many materials that are not named here.

Lumber

The lumber used in most boxes is white pine. It is soft even to the scratch of a fingernail and is very easy for the amateur to use. If you wish to buy new lumber, white pine is good and less expensive than most other kinds--though no lumber is cheap. Beware of oak or other hardwoods on your first attempt!

Composition Boards

Many are the types of composition materials on the present market, each with its own price and particular quality. Here is an explanation of the terms used in the directions given here:

Plywood: Plywood, if bought, is usually rather more expensive than other varieties of composition board. In most cases hardboard could be substituted for it.

Hardboard: Hardboard is the term applied to composition boards with a hard, smooth finish. It is good for construction purposes, although it is somewhat brittle, and very difficult to stick thumbtacks into.

Wallboard: Wallboard is the term applied to the type of composition board that is lightweight, soft, porous--good for bulletin boards or for absorbing sound.

Corrugated cardboard: Many packing boxes are made of it. Heavy noncorrugated cardboard can be used for most of the purposes for which corrugated cardboard is used.

Finishes

Even though scrap materials are suggested, the equipment made need not be shoddy or unattractive. Quite the contrary! The preschool departments of many very well-equipped churches have furniture constructed in this way.

Color Schemes

The same principles of color that apply to the home apply to the church--only more so! There is no special virtue in somber, unimaginative browns. More and more the soft greens, yellows, blues, and pinks are being used as background colors. In painting rooms, a light shade is good; and if possible, the woodwork should be painted to match the walls. Furniture in a natural finish, or painted to harmonize with the walls, is good--painting every chair in the preschool group a different color may create a sense of confusion. Bright accents in a room can come from toys, pictures, and display articles. Furniture in the housekeeping corner should harmonize with other furnishings. If you are doing an extensive redecorating job, you will want to consult someone who knows.

Preparing the Wood

Make the equipment sturdy. Be sure there are no sharp or rough edges; use sandpaper or a file to remove sharp corners. In preschool groups round the edges as far as possible so that children knocking against them will not be harmed. Be sure there are no nails sticking out; either pound them into the wood, take them out and use a shorter nail, or blunt the point by holding a piece of iron--as another hammer--against the point while pounding on the head of the nail. Some of the boxes suggested are made of rather rough or undressed wood. Sand them to remove splinters. If desired, a plane may be used to make the surfaces a little smoother. This is not always worth the trouble.

The Use of Paint

Undressed wood absorbs a great deal of paint on the first coat. Some use a wood sealer such as a mixture of 2/3 shellac and 1/3 alcohol as the first coat; others use a first or prime coat of flat white paint. If your paint has been donated--as much of the paint for these projects will be--it may be just as economical to use the regular paint on the wood as a first coat. Enamel gives a sturdy, glossy finish. Two coats will usually cover any ordinary defects in the wood. Sand the first coat lightly. Rubber-base paint is good to cover up printing and other irregularities on boxes, and makes a nice finish. It is well to use a washable paint so that equipment may be kept clean. Either enamel or rubber-base water paint are washable. If you have new wood, a natural finish is very nice. Further hints on finishing may be picked up from paint stores or carpenters!

Remember, a good paint or plain finish will take away any feeling on the part of some that equipment made of scrap materials is junky.

Be sure to stir paint well before using. Some paint needs to be stirred ten or fifteen minutes to be thoroughly mixed.

Have several layers of paper under the work. Keep a rag wet with turpentine handy, to wipe up any spilled paint immediately so that it will not leave permanent spots.

Care of Brushes

Brushes that have been left in bad condition can often be reclaimed by using an inexpensive commercial brush cleaner available in a variety or paint store.

Always clean the brushes after using them with turpentine, paint thinner, or any similar preparation. Most rubber-base paints can be cleaned from a brush with water. Shellac cannot be cleaned with turpentine, but with an alcohol-base preparation.

Brushes to be used the next day may be kept from drying by wrapping them in aluminum foil. Keep brushes flat or suspended, without weight on bristles.

Paints and painting equipment are a fire hazard. Keep turpentine, brush cleaner, and paints tightly covered. Destroy all paint- or turpentine-soaked rags. Keep painting equipment out of tightly closed cupboards to avoid spontaneous combustion.

CHAPTER

VIII

MAKING GENERAL EQUIPMENT

Equipment Described in This Chapter

COAT RACKS

In each department or room there should be a place for the wraps of those who will use the room on Sundays or weekdays.

Learning to take care of his wraps by himself is a part of the training of a little child. Placing a low stool nearby helps such children to get in and out of overshoes. In many church schools each child has an assigned space for his wraps, marked by a flower or animal sticker. A spring clothespin marked in the same way helps to keep overshoes and mittens together. Hooks are more easily used by the small child; if it is necessary to use hangers on a rod to conserve space, buy wooden ones--and have someone nearby to lend a hand.

Hooks, or rods for hangers, together with shelves for hats, overshoes, and so on, can of course be put in almost any corner as part of the permanent, built-in equipment.

A portable coat rack (see illustration on this page) can easily be made by putting a frame on "feet" and screwing hooks into the top crosspiece. You will need:

2 pieces of wood 1 1/4" x 3" of the height desired for uprights, about 38" for preschool and 5' for adults.

2 pieces 1" x 2" the length desired. A rack is easily movable if the length is not much greater than the height. It is better to set the crosspieces in grooves, if you can find someone with the necessary knowledge and tools. Otherwise use four crosspieces in pairs, nailing them on opposite sides of the upright for balance.

2 pieces for feet; scraps 12" to 15" long.

4 casters.

Do not have hooks too close together; actually try out the space needed for the wraps commonly used in the coldest weather in your area. For children, the crosspiece on which hooks are screwed should be slightly above their eye level. Adding a shelf that projects beyond the hooks provides both eye protection and a place for hats. All portable racks should be on casters for easy moving.

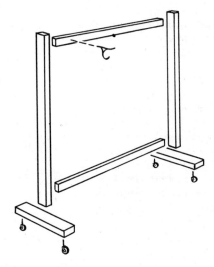

SEATING

When it comes to chairs of the proper sizes for various age groups (see page 47) it is best to buy rather than to attempt to construct them. They should be well designed and sturdy. The making of chairs from orange crates, etc., is hardly worth the time and effort involved.

Possible alternatives are pews (several of which could also be cut "to size"); or, for children, benches, stools, and floor mats. The last three named are described in Chapter IX. They are especially usable for children in the primary and preschool groups.

TABLES

Tables are a very necessary part of church school equipment. Since the purchase of tables represents quite an expense, they should be available for use in more than one group, and for more than one purpose. Tables can be made or purchased with legs that are either adjustable or removable, so that the same tables used for church dinners can also be used when needed for the various age groups. This is simple if the legs are of pipe. Several sets of legs, of different lengths, can be secured. These legs can be screwed in and out of fixtures (technically called "floor flanges") which can be bought at any hardware store or plumber's shop.

Rectangular tables are more usable than round ones and take less space. An easy way to make them is to buy (at a building supply yard) the type of door called a "flush door"--one that has a smooth surface like a table. This can be fitted with legs of pipe as described above.

Tables seating not more than eight pupils--with the teacher sitting toward the middle of one side, not at the end--are the best type. For a large group three or more of them can be arranged in U shape or in a square. Care should be taken that tables are not too heavy to be safely handled by women, or by older boys and girls. Lightweight metal tables that fold into compact units are now available commercially at prices that are sometimes less than the cost of materials to make them. The kind most advertised seat six, and are very easy to handle and to store.

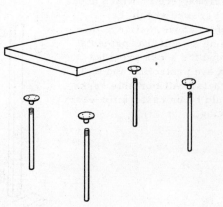

Other Working Surfaces for Pupils

If the room for younger children is not big enough to have both tables and open space, it is much more important to have the open space! Very often the children can use the floor for drawing or for other activities for which a table is ordinarily used. In the one-room church, pew seats make a good working surface, with pieces of cardboard fitted over them for protection. The children can be seated on small benches or stools that can be pushed under the pews when not in use--or can even kneel on the floor. Children also like to use easels for writing and drawing (see pages 82-83).

In classes for older children and young people lapboards can be provided for each pupil when they are to write or draw. A board 12" x 18" is quite satisfactory. For this purpose pieces cut from corrugated cardboard boxes and bound with gummed paper cost almost nothing and with care will last a long time. The corrugated boards that come between large records are excellent for this purpose, and both music stores and individuals will gladly save them for you.

Lapboards cut from plywood, or made of thin hardboard such as masonite, will last indefinitely and take up little storage room. Spring clips will keep the papers from slipping, and pencils can be tied to the clips.

Tables can sometimes be found at auctions or in secondhand stores--or even in the attics of homes. These are usable if not too large or heavy, and they can be cut down to proper heights (see page 47). Painting or staining them to match the room in which they will be used completes the process. In rooms that are very small, a table sometimes gets in the way of a creative program if it takes up most of the space. In such a situation, a table-sized shelf can be hinged to the wall and raised when needed, if portable tables are not at hand. Proper wall brackets for this purpose can be found at hardware stores.

SUPPLY CUPBOARDS

The storage of supplies is a real problem in most churches, but especially so in the small church. Here are some suggestions for storage space.

Good supply cupboards can be made from orange or apple crates, or from any similar wooden boxes, put together in various arrangements.

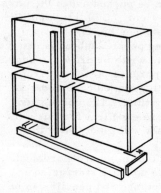

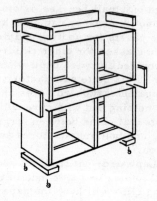

A very simple arrangement of four apple boxes nailed together.

Two orange crates nailed together. Scrap lumber has been used to reinforce the sides; to make supports for casters; to put a rim around the top.

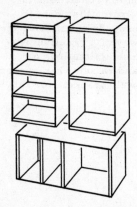

Four orange crates. Two of these were stood upright, with a third crossways, as a base for them. When in place, all were firmly nailed together. Sections from the fourth box were used to make the extra shelves indicated. (See page 77 for a "cutback" design.)

Some professional skill needed, but is neither difficult nor expensive to make under the guidance of a semi-professional carpenter. In one church the tops of such cabinets were covered with hard plastic or linoleum so that during the week the cabinets could be rolled into the kitchen or dining room and used side by side as a working surface.

By having lumber precut, even junior boys can make cabinets such as that shown below, during vacation church school. The materials were as follows (all lumber being soft white pine):

3 pieces 1" x 10", x the <u>length</u> of the shelves desired

1 piece 1" x 10", x 2" longer than these 3 pieces

2 pieces 1" x 10", x the <u>height</u> desired

4 10" lengths of quarter round to use as shelf supports

2 10" lengths of 2" x 4"s for bottom supports for casters

4 casters

4 corner brackets for reinforcing each corner at the back
    Finishing nails

For younger children the back of such a cabinet can be covered with wallboard to be used as a place to display pictures, etc.

The appearance of such cupboards can be improved by using narrow lath to cover all edges and by covering the slatted sides with heavy cardboard before the painting is done. Anyone having a power saw can cut strips that are acceptable substitutes for lath from 1" board. Such cupboards should be painted like, or in harmony with, the wall against which they will stand; or they can be covered (see page 28) with one of the new plastic materials. If desired, curtains can be hung in front of open cabinets, but this is generally found to be more of a nuisance than a help. If other uses of the room make it desirable to hide what is on the shelves at times, it is better to finish the back carefully, put the cupboard on casters, and when it is not in use turn the open side to the wall.

The lumber for such cabinets can be precut in a local lumberyard to exact measurements.

Some children's departments have added onto the end of such cabinets a holder for a roll of paper towels, which are useful in cleanup sessions.

Substitutes for Supply Cupboards

In class groups in which space is very much at a premium, and only paper and small supplies are involved, shoe bags can be furnished with tape loops to hang on anything available--even the back of a chair or pew--to hold crayons, pencils, paintbrushes, etc.

A good holder for papers of all sizes can be made from a long paper bag of the kind that comes from the dry cleaner over clothing. The steps are as follows:

1. Loosen the folded-down corners at the top and even the top off.
2. Fold this open edge over to the back about 2", and paste down. This gives a smooth front surface.
3. Fold up the lower end 8" to form a pocket. Sew or staple the outer edges of this pocket (also the others indicated in 4).
4. At a point 7" above the upper edge of this lowest pocket make a fold, 6" deep, forming a second pocket.
5. At a point 6" above the top edge of this second pocket, make a 3" fold, forming a third shallow pocket. These folds can be varied in size as desired, but the pockets suggested can easily hold papers of standard sizes: beginning at the bottom, 12" x 18" and 9" x 12"; the others, papers of smaller sizes.

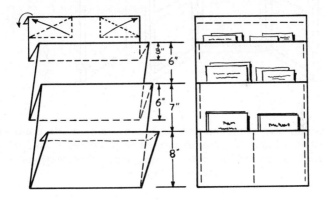

If desired, the whole paper holder can be stapled to a large piece of carton cardboard the size of the finished wall pocket, which adds to its firmness and durability. Such a holder can be used for books by sewing or stapling divisions of the folded pockets. The whole thing can be hung near the place where paper will be needed, or where books are to be displayed.

A window shade can be used in the same way and would be even more durable.

SCREENS AND OTHER PARTITIONS

Since sight is more disturbing to the child than sound, much use can be made of screens for dividing classes that must meet in the same room.

A good screen can be made from two or three sections of a packing crate from large furniture. This crating is usually cardboard with wooden framework. Hinges, purchased or made from scraps of leather such as an old belt, can be used to fasten together the number of screen sections desired. Screens can be painted or covered with wallpaper. Such a screen may be used as a bulletin board, or a substitute for a blackboard (by thumbtacking on it large sheets of newsprint and writing with dark crayons), or to shut off unused space or unsightly equipment. They are not good to use where small children are involved, or to support anything heavy, as wraps, since they are rather easily thrown out of balance.

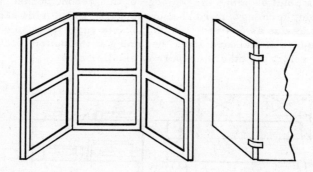

A combination partition and cupboard can be made from crates and a mattress box. If a longer partition is needed, two such cupboards can be used side by side, facing opposite directions and thus providing cupboard space for two classes.

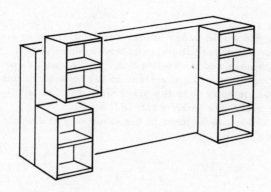

You will need:
   1 cardboard mattress box, double-bed size
   4 orange crates or apple boxes
   Thin nails, 1" to 1 1/2" long, with flat heads
   Circular pieces of tin, with nail holes in center (they are
   usually available wherever furniture or appliances are
   unpacked); or you can use the tops of small tin cans

Nail the crates together in pairs, end to end. Fasten one
pair of crates to each end of the mattress box. Nail from inside
the crates, holding the mattress box firmly in place so the nails
will penetrate. Put a tin disk on each nail inside the mattress
box to keep the cardboard from tearing out. Hammer down the
end of the nail.

A third type of screen (see illustration) has been found very useful. It can be used in a variety of ways to divide groups of any age. For use with young children a 3' or 4' screen is high enough. You will need:

- 2 pieces of wallboard 4' x 6' and approximately 7/8" thick
- About 30' of lumber 2 1/2" to 3" wide and about 1 3/8" thick, grooved to fit the wallboard, as a frame
- 2 pieces of lumber 1" x 3" x 30" for the feet
- 2 pieces 1/4" x 2" x 6' to cover the center seam
- 4 metal shelf brackets--a size large enough to support the screen

This same type of screen has been used successfully also in the church basement for dividing classes. Two screens enclosing a corner make an excellent room, and two set at right angles to a wall with a window make a well-lighted class space. They take little storage room if the feet are overlapped.

The wallboard may be of the soft variety conducive to the use of thumbtacks and masking tape and thus providing a large display area; or it may be a hardboard (masonite) for greater durability. If the screen is to be used for heavy objects (such as wraps hung on a row of hooks), the frame and feet should be of sturdy lumber and well-braced.

The wallboard is a sound deadener.

This screen was made by a "home carpenter" who had basement equipment.

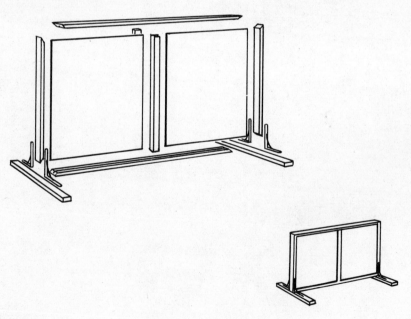

A Hanging Partition

A hanging partition has been used successfully to create temporary rooms in the basement of a small church.

Celotex or some other porous wallboard was set in 1 1/4" x 2" wood frames about 4' x 8' (cut a little less than ceiling height). Two screw hooks were placed in the top of each screen.

The ceiling was marked off according to the floor divisions desired. Screw eyes (about 3/4" opening) were placed in ceiling and 3/8" iron rods run through eyes. The rods and rings were permanent installation. Rods hung about 1" from ceiling.

The screens are hung by the hooks from rods. When unobstructed area is desired for dinner, etc., screens are taken down and stacked in a corner. Changing the screens takes about ten minutes.

This installation has proved to be durable and good-looking.

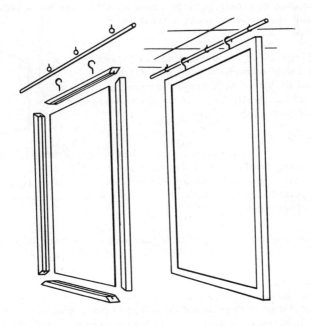

Draperies

Many one-room churches or churches with basements have found draw drapes a real help in forming partitions. If such are installed, be sure to consider the problem of light and air for each class. Passageways should also be considered.

BULLETIN BOARDS

Bulletin boards should be made of material into which thumbtacks may be easily pushed, and should be framed in some way. If painted the same color as the wall, they will usually be acceptable to all using a multi-purpose room. They should be on the eye level of the pupils. The following are ways of making them:

1. Pieces of porous wallboard are sometimes left from building projects and may be had for the asking. A thin molding placed around the board will give a finished appearance.

2. The side of a refrigerator crate may be used for a bulletin board. Paint will make it quite attractive.

3. A large piece of corrugated cardboard from a carton will likewise make a good bulletin board. The edges should be bound with brown gummed paper tape, at least 1" wide. Wallpaper can be used to edge or completely cover such a board.

4. A corrugated box makes a very attractive table-size, triptychlike bulletin board that will stand by itself. It may be edged with wallpaper trim or bound with gummed paper, then painted or stained and coated with clear shellac.

5. A piece of framed wallboard fastened to the back of an upright piano serves many purposes. Placed at right angles to the wall, the piano forms a partition, shutting off a junior committee or a kindergarten interest center as well as providing bulletin board space. Displays need not be removed after each session as they are completely hidden when the piano is pushed back against the wall. If a piano is to be moved often, put oversized rubber casters on it.

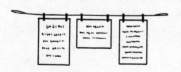

6. A line of wire or heavy cord looped at both ends for easy removal may be stretched along a wall between two hooks. Pictures or displays could be attached with spring clothespins of colored plastic in an attractive manner.

7. A blanket (or any heavy cloth hung over a rope, clothesline fashion) can be used as a way of displaying pictures, maps, and other teaching aids. In the same way, a piece of cloth may be arranged over the back of a chair or pew so that pictures and other display material may be pinned to it.

Bulletin boards may be fastened to the wall, hung from the molding (by molding hooks), placed on an easel, or carried about to lean against a wall or chair back. (See also pages 58 ff.)

TURNOVER CHARTS

Turnover charts are especially handy for displaying the words of hymns and memory Scripture, for freehand map-drawing, and any other teaching method that calls for display before a whole class or department. Among the ways of making them are the following:

1. One type of very simple chart is made in the same way as the picture display stand described on page 69, made from large pieces of cardboard, such as those which come with curriculum picture sets.

2. Commercial turnover charts may often be obtained after their use has been fulfilled, and the back of the sheets may be used for the printing of charts, since the back sheets are usually plain. (Some churches use such charts in certain of their promotion programs.)

3. This is a portable chart rack that is easily made. You will need:

    2   4 1/2' uprights (or any desired height) of 1 1/2" x 1 1/2" lumber

    8   7" pieces of scrap lumber (about 1" x 3") for feet

    1   crosspiece (1" dowel or a broomstick) about 3' to 4' long (or desired length)

    16   screws (1 1/2" to 2")

    2   clamps (of the kind to hold a broom to the wall)

    2   shower curtain or notebook rings to hang charts

Screw 4 of the feet to each upright in the manner shown in the illustration. Two screws will hold each board firmly to the upright, holding much more firmly than nails. Fasten broomstick clamps at equal distances from the top of each upright (about 3" from the top). Fasten these to the uprights sidewise rather than up and down.

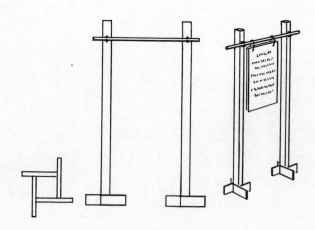

4. Ready-made frames for large charts can often be found in stores that have commercial displays that need to be turned frequently. Paint stores also have such charts. Often such frames can be obtained for the asking when the purpose of the charts has been served.

5. An excellent turnover chart rack can be made with pipe.

Use ordinary plumbing pipe in whatever size it is cheapest (probably 1/2"). You will need:

1   pipe 24" to 30" (depending on the width paper you intend
        to use)
2   pipes 54" long
6   90-degree els
2   T joints
4   pipes 9" long

Have threads cut on both ends of each piece of pipe (perhaps a plumber in your church will sell the pipe at cost and cut it for you). Clean the pipes with solvent, if necessary.

By hand or with a pipe wrench, put the pipes together to make a frame on a standard.

Paint if desired. Be sure to remove all rust first, if you are using an old pipe. A special kind of paint can be bought with a base that makes it stick to metal. Ask your dealer for further information about it.

Punch holes in the charts and fasten them to the rack with 2" notebook rings. (Directions for making charts to be used on these racks may be found on page 72.)

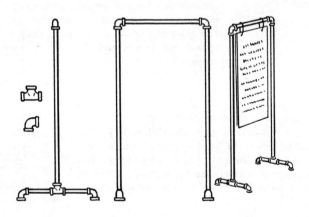

BLACKBOARDS AND OTHER WRITING SURFACES

It is very difficult to make a satisfactory chalkboard, though hardboard painted with blackboard paint has been used. Very often blackboards can be secured from old schoolhouses being sold because of consolidation. Blackboards can be purchased at not too great an expense. It is recommended that they be portable, for a permanent blackboard on a wall makes it difficult to do anything else with that wall. The blackboard is not a recommended piece of equipment for preschool groups.

A substitute writing surface can be made by thumbtacking several sheets of paper (newsprint or roll wrapping or shelf paper) to a large piece of corrugated cardboard from a carton, using dark crayons as a writing medium. This can even be held on a teacher's lap, although slanting it slightly against some form of support is better. The larger heavy cardboard stand-up advertisements make good portable writing surfaces of this kind. Two such surfaces, hinged loosely with masking tape, can be placed over the back of a pew.

DISPLAY EQUIPMENT FOR BOOKS

Books are important teaching tools, and their care and display is often sadly neglected. To be of use they must be readily available; to get them read, they must be attractively displayed.

Books may of course be kept in any of the cupboard space described on pages 54 to 59. For older children, young people, or adults open bookshelves are easily devised.

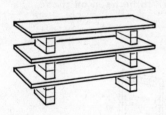

Begin with heavy 10" boards of any desired shelf length. Stack them in the shelf heights needed by supports of: bricks, hollow tile, cement blocks and so on, with each shelf extending several inches beyond its support. The boards should be sanded; they can also be painted or stained if desired, as can the supports.

A holder of transparent plastic material made like a shoe bag is also useful for displaying books. In making such a holder, plan carefully for pockets the width of the books to be displayed, and a little more than half their height. This takes little space and can be hung on a chair back or pew. When the books are removed it can be folded and put away.

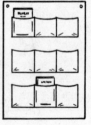

A pew or low table is an important part of a book center, with a few chairs, benches, or stools of proper height. A few books closely associated with the teaching purpose of the day can be arranged on the table, with others between book ends or on shelves for free choice.

Bookrack

Such a rack is made from crating from a large piece of furniture, which is usually cardboard with a wooden frame.

Fit the piece of crating into slots made in (or nail its base between) several blocks of wood, heavy and large enough to serve as substantial feet for the rack, so it will stand up. At the upper edge of the base and across the center of this frame nail a 3" or 4" board of the same length, slanting each one slightly by inserting wedge-shaped pieces at each end (such wedges can be obtained at a furniture store as they are used to brace furniture when it is packed for shipment; or they are easily made by sawing a cube of wood cornerwise).

The slanted boards provide space for displaying books, open or closed. The entire rack serves as a partition to shut off a quiet corner for book browsing.

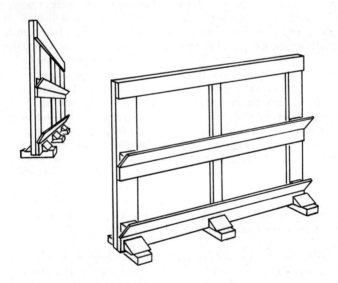

Book Ends

Book ends are very helpful in keeping books straight on shelves, standing upright on display tables, and in good condition generally.

Bricks--either common building bricks or glass bricks--may be used for book ends. The bricks may also be painted with enamel or rubber-base paint, or covered with a material such as one of the imitation leathers made from plastic. Old-fashioned sadirons painted in shiny black or gay colors make sturdy book ends.

PICTURES
Mounting

Pictures, large and small, are an important teaching tool. If properly cared for and filed, they can be quickly located when needed, and used over and over.

The first step is proper care in mounting pictures, to protect the edges and display them more effectively. Construction paper, tagboard, or lightweight cardboard (about 3 ply) give enough protection for average use. Allow for at least an inch-wide border at top and sides, and twice that at the bottom of the picture. Shirt cardboards make good mountings for the smaller pictures found in magazines and catalogues, or purchased from publishers of inexpensive prints. A thin mucilage or paste is best for this purpose, coating the picture, rather than the mounting. The safest way to proceed is to place the upper corners of the picture in the exact position desired, pressing down and out with a soft, clean cloth. Work out all wrinkles quickly; and be sure the corners are tightly pasted.

A sticker on which is written the name of the picture, the artist (if known), a file number or name, and any other information that is useful to you may be pasted on the back of the mounting; also a gummed cloth hanger if desired. Such hangers are available in stationery and variety stores.

For your better, larger, or more frequently used pictures, a mounting of masonite or plywood can be used, or an inexpensive frame made or bought. A frame should be fitted with a removable backing, with butterfly latches so the picture in it can be changed. This is particularly desirable in using teaching pictures from a set of the same size. Clear shellac is a good protection for a picture permanently mounted, rather than glass.

Displaying

Pictures should be displayed at about the eye level of the age group involved. They should be used in many ways and places, and at appropriate times, rather than hung in large numbers all at once.

For lightweight pictures, masking tape is safe on most surfaces; Scotch tape is not. For small children the back of a chair or pew can be used for displaying a picture or pictures. For any age, single pictures or a group can be hung--with spring-type clothespins--on a taut wire or heavy cord stretched between hooks or other supports on the wall or even between the backs of two heavy chairs.

The cardboard backs between which the teaching pictures of a set are shipped provide a way to display, protect, and transport them.

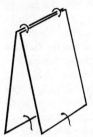

Put loose-leaf rings through the top of both cardboards and a tie cord through the other ends. The cardboards can then be stood on a table in V effect, forming a support for the picture being shown. The addition of blotter corners or corners made from heavy envelopes to the cardboards will hold the picture in place. Heavy cardboards used for advertising displays in stores can be used in the same way. Cover them with plain cloth, or with a coat of paint and shellac, and you will have additional folders to store, transport, and display pictures, maps, charts, memory Scripture, or the words of hymns. For a more permanent turnover chart see page 65.

Easels provide another way to display such materials, especially pictures. Three kinds--each one easy and inexpensive to make--can fill every need. Cut a newspaper pattern following the general lines in the illustration, in any desired size (a 14" height, with each arm 9" is a good size for quite large pictures); this proportion must be maintained in any size easel, for balance.

1. The small size, to be used for small, lightweight pictures, can be cut from a file folder, or from any cardboard light enough to fold.

Both the small and large sizes can also be made from:

2. The corners of large cardboard cartons, each carton making four. Strengthen them by covering the edges with brown gummed paper and coating the whole with shellac or wood stain.

3. Plywood scraps, cutting the two sides and hinging them together with small brass hinges. Plywood (3/8") will hold a very large, heavy picture. A coat of shellac, wood stain, or paint makes a nice finish.

One ingenious man fastened two long strips of molding (of a "stand-out" type) to the wall, spaced so that it was possible to slip pictures from the set in and out. A piece of glass or sheet cellophane cut to proper size can be slipped in also, to protect the pictures.

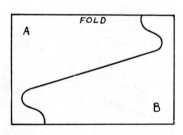

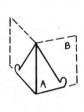

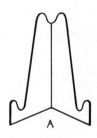

Filing

A good file box for pictures can be made from large cardboard or wooden boxes, carefully chosen as to size; or can be easily constructed to the measurements desired. Such a box file should be placed on a low table, on sturdy legs, or on a wooden platform, in each case making the top of the box come about waist high. Casters are desirable for easy moving about. The boxes can be made to file the pictures vertically or horizontally, the former perhaps being best for the usual teaching picture sets, in order to see the subject readily. The box should be about two inches higher than the pictures to be filed to allow space for cardboard or wooden divisions and subject indicator tabs. It should be just wide enough to slip the division boards and pictures in and out easily. Indicator tabs can be made from large gummed stickers or from heavy gummed paper. They should be staggered for easy reading (see illustration).

Some teachers prefer a flat file such as is shown in the illustration. This type takes more careful construction. A good carpenter can groove the sides of the file in such a way that the divisions slide in and out.

Such file cases can be made and used for posters, flat maps, charts of the words of Scripture or hymns, handwork patterns--in fact, anything that you want to keep and have readily available. Any picture or article to be filed should be marked with its proper file number, always placed in the same relative position on the back (as, in the upper righthand corner) for quick and accurate refiling. The categories for filing should be those most useful to you. In general, however, the following have been found good for pictures from the sets:

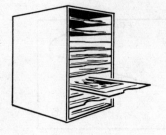

Bible Background	Community Helpers
Customs	
The Land	Jesus
	Nativity
Children	Childhood
In Groups	Deeds
Alone	Teaching
Of Other Lands and Races	Holy Week
Church, The	Nature
Families at Church	
In the Church School	Old Testament
The World Church	(Subdivided as used)

These are main categories, in which subdivisions can be made as your collections grow.

More ambitious suggestions for file cases include a hassock type, with a slip cover and cushion of one of the plastic leatherette materials; a reconstructed record cabinet; verticle shelves, 2, 3 and 4 inches apart, set in discarded chest; and many others. The sky, apparently, is the limit.

MAKING MAPS

Maps are most useful in the church school teaching of older children, young people, and adults. They can be made by juniors or young people from any good Bible atlas, in any size desired. A pantograph to accurately enlarge small maps could probably be borrowed from a local school; if not, any teacher knows how to enlarge maps by the squared-off method.

Maps can be drawn or painted on:

1. Window shades--of paper or linen, in a light color. As in the case of charts, if the same size shade is used for all maps, a shade fixture on the wall provides a good display method. Tag each map so it need not be unrolled to be identified.

2. Sign linen--the material on which commercial painters make signs. Available where paint supplies are sold, this material has a very smooth surface, is easy to use with crayons or paint, and rolls well.

3. White cotton feed sacks or old sheets. These must be stretched firmly during the drawing or painting process. They can be put in a frame if desired.

4. Walls. Such maps make a colorful decoration, and if done with waterpaint, can be removed or painted over easily. Permission from the proper authority for this is necessary, of course.

5. Large sheets of cardboard, or paper fastened to such sheets for firmness.

MAKING CHARTS

The charts to be used on turnover racks, or in other ways, can be made from a variety of materials. Cardboard is good, but rather expensive in quantity. The backs of advertising cardboards from local stores are a possibility, also large sheets of wrapping or shelf paper, or the paper from dry cleaning bags. Pieces of old sheets cut to desired size and hemmed have been used, as have window shades. If a standard size of shade is available cheaply, your rack can be a regular shade holder, fastened to the wall from which they are to be displayed. These shades, if white, can be used to project slides or filmstrips in small groups.

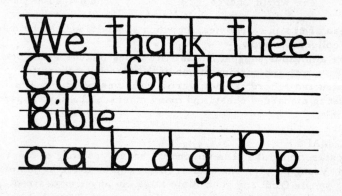

The lettering on charts should be that used for each age group in the local schools. Lettering can be done with wax crayons or with any of the commercial lettering pens and pencils, now available in various colors. The sample lettering given above is commonly used in the second grade.

CHURCH SCHOOL RECORDS

Both current and permanent church school records should be carefully kept and should be available for use by proper officers in a central place. Types of record books are numerous, and should be chosen to fit your particular needs. But whatever your record system, a closet or cabinet with adequate shelf space and a lock should be provided. Although any staff member should have access promptly to needed information, only the secretary or treasurer should be allowed to handle the records. Thoroughness and accuracy are of great importance if good use is to be made of such records, and if necessary information is to be available to the superintendent, the minister, and succeeding officers.

WORSHIP EQUIPMENT

In Chapter IV, page 23, reference is made to a possible need for a background for worship and other general group activities for which concentrated attention is desired.

One such background can be a large three-leaf screen (sometimes called a triptych) such as that described on page 58. It should be made in such a way that pictures, maps, or charts can be displayed on each leaf as necessary. It is most effective if painted or stained the color of the wall or woodwork, or a dark, rich contrasting color. A flat screen of the type described on page 59 can also be used for this purpose.

A larger frame of pipe, made in the same way as the turnover chart rack on page 65, can be used as a support for heavy curtains for such a background. A neutral color is best for this purpose.

It is wise to omit all ecclesiastical symbols from such backgrounds.

FOR CLEANING UP

Wastebaskets can be made from almost any kind of container, from cardboard cartons to oil cans. The main point in a church school in which the boys and girls are "learning by doing" is to have enough of them readily accessible, of good size, attractively painted or covered in some way, and frequently emptied!

When work is being done with materials that are messy, it is wise to have facilities for washing hands near the work. They may consist simply of a washbasin, plus No. 10 cans for fresh and waste water, a roll of paper toweling, and a wastebasket for soiled towels. A child will be better able to use an adult-sized washbasin in the lavatory if a sturdy step is provided.

Running water for the washing of hands during a vacation church school or even a Sunday church school session that has access to the outdoors can come from a No. 10 can. Near the bottom a small hole made with a nail is plugged with a matchstick when not in use. The matchstick is tied to the handle, as is the soap. The wire handle can be used for hanging the watering can to a tree or post. Paper towels can be kept or hung nearby. In one vacation church school there was enough water from a single filling of such a can to wash the hands of seventy children at recess. A teacher or older child stood nearby to help the younger children.

CHAPTER

IX

MAKING PRESCHOOL EQUIPMENT

All of the articles described in the previous chapter are not only useful but necessary in the preschool, and there is only the matter of adaptation to the proper sizes (see page 47) and use. In the main, they are made according to the same directions except where otherwise indicated. Be especially careful, if using old materials, to plane or sand rough splintery surfaces to be sure there are no protruding nails, and to round corners wherever possible. Use hard-finish, nonchipping paints. Look back over Chapter VIII, the sections on:

Coat racks   Screens
Seating   Bulletin boards
Tables, etc.   Bookracks, etc.
Supply cupboards   Pictures

In this chapter you will find directions for making:

BENCHES AND STOOLS
Because of the informal nature of the program with preschool children, it is not necessary to have a chair for each child. This is particularly true in crowded situations, for it is much more important to have space in which to move from one activity to another. The children may sit on the floor on pads (see page 82) or roll-up rugs for a story period.

A stool can be made by sawing a nail keg to the desired height. The wire that is around the keg near each end supports the boards of the keg sufficiently. Make a pad and valance (or skirt) for the stool of oilcloth, cloth, or some other material. For older children for whom the keg is the right height, pad the top and paint the keg.

A simple bench for one child can be made from scrap lumber. Such a bench is very useful in the housekeeping corner, or near the place where wraps are removed.

Wooden boxes such as shot boxes and dynamite boxes make good benches as do large hollow blocks. No. 10 cans and 5-quart oil cans can be fitted with pads and valances in the same manner as the nail kegs.

DOLL BEDS

Doll beds may be of many varieties and sizes according to the amount of space available and the sizes and numbers of the dolls. Where there is ample space, a doll bed large enough for children is quite to their liking, so that they can play at being "the baby."

1. Use: 1 large box (fish box or fruit lug) turned upside down. Piece of plywood sawed to fit end of box and to extend several inches above it. Nail or screw this headboard on the box.
   Tufted mattress made to fit.
   Washable bedspread, pillow, and sheets.

2. Use: A box such as a Tokay grape box (fruit lug), open side up. Large spools or wooden blocks can be fastened at each corner as legs.

A small bed will fit under a pew in a one-room church, or will take up little space in a cupboard.

A small mattress and bedding placed on a pew or chair can also serve as a doll bed.

TEA TABLE

(This table is for the housekeeping center. For larger worktables, see page 52.)

1. Use: 3 Tokay grape boxes (or any similar boxes, provided they are identical).

Plywood or boards to form the table top, a little wider than the boxes.

Place the two boxes upright (open sides out) and nail the table top on them. The open edge of each box should be almost flush with the top, thus serving as legs for the table. Use the ends of the third box to insert an extra shelf in each "leg" for storing dishes. Another board nailed between the boxes toward the bottom will give support.

2. Use: 1 apple box or orange crate

1 wide board for the table top, of plywood or hardboard (masonite). An old wooden breadboard is good.

Stand the box or crate upright, cutting it down to height if necessary. To do this carefully, remove the top (one end) by pulling the nails; mark evenly around the box the desired height and saw off at that line; renail the top for extra firmness; nail the new top in place. Sand both the box and the new top if necessary before painting. It is easier also to paint the base before putting on the table top.

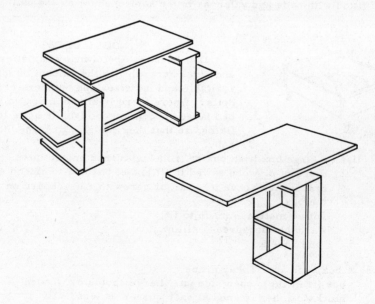

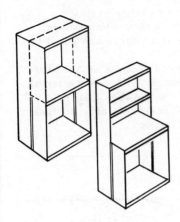

DISH CABINET

Use: 1 orange crate, standing on end.

Saw away one half the top and one half each side down to the center division board. You now have a full-size lower compartment and a "cutback" upper section, like a Dutch cupboard. Use the top of the removed half of the crate as an additional shelf for this upper section. An end or center division of another crate may be used as a shelf in the lower section also.

Wallboard or heavy cardboard fitted across the back before painting will make a neater finish, as will narrow lath along the edges.

STOVE

Use: 2 apple boxes

Drawer pull (this may be a spool or wooden bead)

Door catch

Lightweight hinges (2 pieces of leather will do)

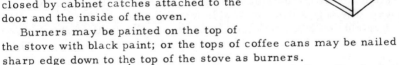

Stand one box upright to form the outer walls of the stove. Use the ends of the other box for the bottom and door of the oven. The bottom of the oven is nailed in like a shelf and the door is hinged to it. The oven handle should be fastened near the top of this door, which is held closed by cabinet catches attached to the door and the inside of the oven.

Burners may be painted on the top of the stove with black paint; or the tops of coffee cans may be nailed sharp edge down to the top of the stove as burners.

If desired, a board could be attached to extend about five inches above the stove at the back, and spools or door buttons nailed to the board to be used to "turn the burner on."

SINK

Use: 2 boxes such as apple boxes or orange crates

1 galvanized pan, at least 5" deep, rectangular in
shape (refrigerator pans or roasters are good) and
as wide as the box tops

4 boards as long as the finished sink, to be used for
supports at the top and bottom. This is the length
of the two boxes with the pan between them

Covering for the top of the sink--preferably linoleum

Broom tick for drying rod (optional)

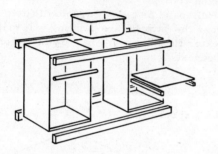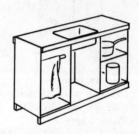

Be sure to check the height of the finished sink against the proper working surface height for the children with whom you are working (see page 47). If orange crates are used, they will probably have to be cut down. If apple boxes are used, they may be increased in height by a board or blocks on the bottom.

Place the pan between the boxes. Since most pans have two rims, it will probably need no more support than the two boards that will be nailed across the back at top and bottom to hold the boxes together. The pan is thus removable for emptying.

The sink may be made more attractive by fastening lightweight linoleum with linoleum paste on the tops of the crates; a very good grade of oilcloth can also be used.

Metal edging or 1/2" round edging around the linoleum will give the sink a more finished look. Be sure all corners of the metal edging are smooth.

Extra shelves in the supporting boxes and a rod for drying dish cloths will add to the sink's usefulness. Such a rod can be cut from a broomstick and nailed inside the box like a clothes hanger rod.

A good addition would be a piece of plywood or other board placed to extend across the back and above the surface of the sink about 5 inches. Discarded faucets attached to this board will give a realistic effect.

IRONING BOARD

Use: 2 Tokay grape boxes
             1 board shaped as the top of an ironing board, 6" to
               8" longer than the box and about 8" wide
             Cloth for the ironing board pad and cover

Adjust the height of one box (see page 47) to the right working height for children.

Use the ends of the other box to make shelves in the first, on which to place the iron and clothing.

Nail the ironing board to the top of the box. Make a pad and cover that can be tacked on or tied on by tapes.

DRESSER

Use: 2 orange crates cut to the right height
             1 mirror, full-length for children (about twice the
               height of the boxes)

Stand the two crates upright with the mirror between them. Nail a piece of plywood or heavy cardboard across the entire back of the crates and lower part of the mirror, adding an extra piece back of the upper part of the mirror for reinforcement and a better finish.

Cut a piece of plywood the width of the mirror and about 5" high to fasten in front of mirror at the bottom to keep children from kicking mirror.

Use the shelves for clothes to "dress up" in, for doll clothes, and so on.

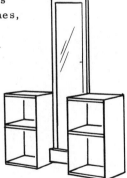

"HOUSE" SCREEN

A folding screen can be used to divide a housekeeping corner from the rest of the room--either the 2-leaf or 3-leaf type. Be sure it is sturdy enough or well enough braced so there is no danger of its falling. Opening, for a door and windows (with curtains!) will add reality.

 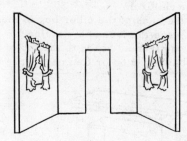

READING CENTER

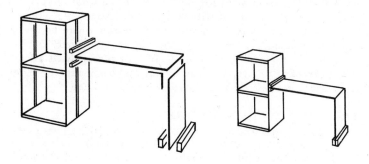

Use: 1 orange crate
            1 piece of lumber 3' long, 10" wide, 3/4" thick
            1 piece 20" long, 3/4" thick
            2 pieces 1" x 1", width of orange crate to support
               shelf
            2 pieces 2" x 4", width of the short board
            2 metal shelf brackets (from variety or hardware store)

Fasten the first two pieces of lumber together at right angles, using the brackets as braces.

Nail the short side between the 2" x 4"s, which will form a solid base for this support.

Fasten a 1" x 1" to the side of the crate so that the 3' board when resting on it will be level, forming a table top. Nail the other one just above, making a groove into which the table top fits snugly, and yet not so tight that it cannot be removed.

Sand and paint or stain the reading center.

Books may be kept in the orange crate, with some displayed on the attached table. Chairs, stools, or benches should be placed on either side of the table.

REST PADS

In preschool groups it is desirable to have times for rest in a lying-down position. Children may bring washable rugs or blankets or large towels from home for this purpose. A simple pad can be made by putting several thicknesses of newspaper in a bag in which dry cleaning has been returned. The newspaper can be kept in place by stitching on a sewing machine or by hand in several places. Paste a picture on the bag near one end for identification. Always fold with the picture side in to make distribution easy and to keep the resting side clean.

SITTING PADS

Since the floor is often used for sitting to listen to stories, sitting pads may be desired, particularly if the floor is not otherwise well protected and clean. Pads for this purpose can be made from the same materials as the rest pads, but need be only 24" square. Enclosing them in pieces of oilcloth or plastic will add to the life of the pads and to the ease of keeping them clean. These are easily stored on shelves or in boxes when not in use.

PAINTING EASELS

An important activity of preschool--and older--groups is easel painting. Since the paper used by the children should be at least 12" x 18"--preferably 18" x 24"--the easel should be at least 4" wider and longer than the paper used. A very simple easel (see illustration) can be made from two pieces of heavy carton cardboard hinged together by masking tape at the top, and fastened with tape or tied at the sides so as to regulate the slant of the easel. The paper can be held to the surface of the easel with thumbtacks or masking tape. The middle of the paper should be at an easy working height for the child. Newsprint is good paper for painting as is cream or white wrapping paper. The paint used is usually powdered tempera.

A good holder for jars of paint is the metal or cardboard holder for six soft drinks. Get jelly or other jars to fit the cartons, and the paints will not fall over and can be carried about without spilling.

For a paint jar holder, the boxlike ends of plate glass crates are good.

Another easel can be made from a chair (usually one can be found fit only for this use). A piece of plywood or heavy corrugated cardboard can be cut to the chair width and placed on a slant from the top of the chair back to about the center of the seat to form a surface on which paper can be thumbtacked. A strip of wood nailed across the seat at this point will support the board, and leave space in front for paint jars which can be placed in the cardboard or wooden holders mentioned above. The holders should be tacked or nailed to the chair.

A series of easels can be made by fastening a wooden shelf 12" wide and any desired length to a wall. This can be hinged or rest

on brackets so it can be put out of the way. A little in front of
center of this board a wooden strip or molding can be added, to
hold easel boards that are slanted against the wall. As in the illustration, the space in front is used for paint jars, preferably in a
holder. Molding strips at the front and side edges of the board will
hold jars or containers in place.

Easels such as the one below are used in many kindergarten
and nursery schools. Since making one takes more than beginning
skill, no directions are given here. A good carpenter could copy
one.

A wooden clothes drying rack makes a good drying rack for
paintings.

Aprons to be used while painting can be made from men's old
shirts from which the sleeves have been cut. These are buttoned
up the back when put on children.

BLOCKS

Large blocks are much easier for children to handle than are the small ones. Birch, pine, and poplar are lightweight woods usable for blocks. Use 2" x 4" lumber, which actually measures 1 3/4" x 3 5/8". A brick or unit will be exactly 7 1/4" long. Scraps of such lumber may be found around the home, on construction projects, in carpenter shops. Measure them, take to a carpenter who has a power saw for quick cutting, and sand each block carefully to remove splinters. These need not be painted to be delightful to the children. If desired, a floor sealer or wax will make a nice finish.

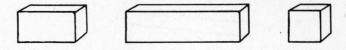

The larger hollow blocks are also good for children to use, and double as stools. These blocks can be made from plywood or hardboard as follows:

Use hard, but not too heavy, lumber, plywood or hardboard, and smooth all surfaces. The two opposite ends of each block are left open, or grooves are cut for lifting. Paint or varnish the blocks. Usable sizes are:

8" x 8" x 8"	8" x 4" x 16"
8" x 4" x 8"	8" x 8" x 16"

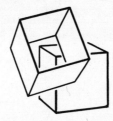

Commercial wooden boxes of sizes similar to those indicated will also serve as blocks, if the lids are nailed on. They include cigar boxes, bullet boxes, dynamite boxes, rectangular cheese boxes.

BLOCK PLAY FIGURES

Children like to play with figures of families, people of Bible lands, helpers such as the postman, and animals. Such figures may be found in kindergarten materials from various denominational boards, in children's cutout and coloring books, and in old dress pattern books.

Paste the figure on a piece of wood (household cement or rubber cement works better than library paste), cut it out with a coping saw, sandpaper to remove rough edges, and coat it with clear shellac. If thin plywood is used, a block of wood should be tacked to the bottom of the figure to make it stand up. If 1" lumber is used, the figure will usually stand alone. To save time, fix a number of figures and ask a carpenter with a power jig saw to cut them out for you.

RHYTHM INSTRUMENTS

Rhythm instruments will add much enjoyment in nursery or kindergarten. They can be used as effectively in the small church as in the large, though they will need to be used softly if in the same room with other classes. They are excellent for the class meeting out of doors and may be kept in a basket for ready transportation.

Rhythm sticks: Cut 12" lengths of 3/8" dowel (hardware store or lumberyard). Broomsticks are not bad! Have enough pairs for a majority of the children.

Bells: Buy jingle bells (especially plentiful at variety stores during the Christmas season) and sew them on wide tape or 1/2" elastic bands to be put on the children's wrist. Bells are also effective tied to the strings of a dish mop!

Sand blocks: Cover the bottom of two blocks of wood about 4" x 5" x 1" with sandpaper. A spool, half a spool, or a cupboard doorknob will make a good handle, fastening one to the opposite side of the block from each sandpaper surface. These surfaces, rubbed together, make the sound.

Rattles: Cover a small tin box (as from Band-Aids) with bright paper or paint. Experiment for different rattling sounds by using inside the box a few beans, tacks, rice, or paper clips. Fasten the top with Scotch tape or masking tape.

Cymbals: Two utensil lids that have wooden knobs.

Drums: A No. 19 can from which both ends have been removed makes a good base for a drum. Pieces of inner tubing are stretched over the ends and laced in the manner of the drawing. Heavy material such as canvas may be used instead and shellacked after it is in place to make it stiff. Sticks, either plain or padded on the end with inner tubing may be used for drumsticks; hands are an acceptable substitute.

Triangles: Buy some common nails, 30-, 40-, and 60-penny size (4 1/2" to 6" in length). Place a loop of yarn, ribbon, or string around the head of the nail and draw it tight. Then tie the other end to a wooden spool. The child holds the spool and strikes the freely hanging nail with another nail.

TOYS

Several satisfactory toys can be made from scrap materials.

Nests of tin cans that will fit into each other make good toys for small children. The cans should be open at one end, making sure there are no sharp edges. Cans may be painted different colors, with enamel paint.

Small children like to place clothespins on the rim of a can. A No. 10 can and wooden clothespins of the nonspring variety can meet this need. The can and the ends of the pins may be painted bright colors.

Spools may be strung on a shoestring in the place of wooden beads. The spools may be dipped in regular dyes.

A train can be made using flat pieces of wood (about 1" x 3" x 8") enameled in gay colors. Place screw hooks and eyes on these blocks so they can be fastened together to form a long train. Wheels are not needed here to make a delightful toy for small children. Attach a string to the front car so the train can be pulled.

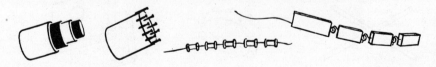

CHAPTER

X

SCRAP MATERIALS

The materials listed here are by no means the only ones that can be used effectively in the making of equipment or in the Christian education program of the church. This list is presented with the hope that it will stimulate the creative use of scrap materials that may be available to you in your particular locality.

MATERIALS	WHERE AVAILABLE	PURPOSE
Wooden boxes, such as are used for oranges, apples, tomatoes, fish	grocery stores	housekeeping furniture, such as supply cabinets, doll beds, ironing board, sink, stove
Tokay grape boxes (fruit lugs)		
Bullet (or shot) boxes	hardware stores Army surplus stores	stools hollow blocks
Dynamite boxes	mining or road construction	
Crating from refrigerators or other large furniture (cardboard with wooden frames)	appliance stores furniture stores	screens bulletin boards
Crating from plate glass	building supply stores	good smooth lumber for making stools, tables, painting easels, etc.
Pipe	plumbers scrap demolition jobs	table legs chart racks

MATERIALS	WHERE AVAILABLE	PURPOSE
Mirrors	homes	dressers
Nail kegs	hardware stores lumberyards	stools
Compound kegs	restaurants creameries	wastebaskets stools
Cardboard packing boxes mattress covers, etc.	furniture stores	bulletin boards floor mats lapboards partitions, etc.
Scrap lumber	building projects woodworking shops lumberyards school manual training shops	2" x 4"s may be cut into block units 1" lumber used for making block play figures and other equipment
Refrigerator pan or other rectangular pan at least 5" deep	hardware store home	sink
Giant ice-cream cartons		wastebaskets
Large 3- or 4-leaf display screens from commercial displays	paint stores appliance stores	screens for church school
Large commercial turnover charts		turnover charts chart racks

Small Items Useful in Construction Which Can Usually Be Found Around the Home

Scraps of hardware: nails, screws, hinges, drawer pulls, hooks, locks, casters, wire
Rope for handles, leather straps for hinges
Linoleum scraps, linoleum paste, metal edging for top of sink and tables
Broom and mop handles for rhythm sticks, coat and chart rods
Scraps of inner tubing for ends of drums
Plastic fabrics to cover bricks for book ends
Glass jars to hold nails of various sizes
Paint: rubber-base, enamel, wood stains

Materials That Can Be Used in Activities in the Church School

MATERIALS	THEIR USE
Tin cans of all sizes (edges smooth)	nests of cans (a toy); paint containers; toy dishes
Food cans with labels still on (open end at bottom of can)	housekeeping corner or store
No. 5 cans	punch holes in top for scissors holder, vases
No. 10 cans	containers for clay; pails for supplies; wash pans
Coffee cans (other cans with lids)	containers for clay, dough, finger paint
Small frozen juice cans	holder for 8 crayons
Cylindrical ice-cream boxes	holders for pencils, crayons
Window shades	charts, maps, screens for projecting films
Old dress pattern books	source of pictures of people for block play figures
Cylindrical boxes (salt, oatmeal)	rhythm instruments
Plastic bags	keep dough, clay, moist; use for display of seed pods and other nature materials
Rolls of wallpaper	cover cardboard screens; use the back for murals, and for art work
Yarn and ribbon	making books; hanging things; weaving
Twine	clothesline in housekeeping corner
Spools	for stringing on shoestrings; making toys; for drawer pulls

MATERIALS	THEIR USE
Metal boxes of all sizes (aspirin on up)	holding small treasures; rhythm instruments
Newspapers	tearing (small children); putting under messy work; stuffing for floor mats; papier-mache; painting
Small bells	rhythm instruments
Paper dry cleaning bags	making floor mats, paper holders (see page 57), song charts
Cardboard easels (stand-up advertisements)	holders for song charts; painting easels
Shirt cardboards	mounting pictures; making books
Wooden clothes driers	drying paintings
Wearing apparel	costumes; dress-up play
Men's shirts	aprons for painting (cut out sleeves, button up the back)
Cold cream jars	paste containers
Sponges	cleanup
Sticks from ice-cream bars or Popsicles	paste sticks
Kitchen equipment pots and pans, rolling pins, egg beaters, cookie cutters, covered refrigerator dishes	housekeeping corner keeping supplies, as clay, crayons
Lids	rhythm instruments
Shoe bags	holding small toys and supplies, doll clothes, books

MATERIALS	THEIR USE
Clothespins, spring type	to hold paper on easels; hang pictures on a wire; keep clothes on line in housekeeping corner; keep pairs of overshoes and mittens together

Pieces of cloth
  rags
  old sheets
  feed sacks
	cleanup ; making wall hangings, doll clothes, doll bed, tablecloths, costumes, drapery materials

Oilcloth, plastic material	table covering, under painting or other art work; cover mats to lie or sit upon; cover nail kegs for stools
Wire glass trays or soft-drink containers	hold paint jars to keep from spilling
Small glass jars	hold paint for art work
Rollers from adhesive tape or electric cord	roll toys
Old clocks	housekeeping play
Magazines	pictures; slick paper for finger painting
Materials for browsing corner, such as magnets, bells (bicycle, door), birds' nests, seed pods, rocks, shells, feathers, magnifying or reading glass	to teach children of God's world

APPENDIX

TO PURCHASE EQUIPMENT

The types of equipment described in this book are available from commercial sources if you prefer to buy ready-made equipment. Consult your denominational headquarters or the local public-school authorities for the names of reliable firms.

SOME HELPFUL BOOKS

Since all this has been directed toward what we speak about as "activity teaching," you may find that you want to learn more about the whole matter. If so, here are some helpful books, all of which are available through your denominational bookstores:

> Creative Activities, by Rebecca Rice. The Pilgrim Press. $3.50.
> Activities in Child Education, by Elizabeth M. Lobingier. The Pilgrim Press. $3.50.
> Here's How and When, by Armilda B. Keiser. Friendship Press. $2.75.
> Make It Yourself, by Bernice W. Carlson. Abingdon Press. $2.00.
> Aim Your Activities at Teaching Religion. A series of very helpful reprints from the International Journal of Religious Education, consisting of eleven articles by Mrs. August Beck. Available from the National Council of Churches, 79 E. Adams Street, Chicago 3, Ill., at 35 cents per set.
> You Can Do It. A booklet published by the American Baptist Publication Society, with a very fine introduction to the whole subject of activity teaching. Largely pictorial. 60 cents.

FOR TRAVELING TEACHERS

If you are concerned with training others for teaching, and have to face the problem of carrying equipment from place to place with you, you may be interested in what one such leader has evolved to put in a 21" suitcase. This has to do with demonstration of an activity type of program for a preschool group, where the only space is between two pews, turned to face each other.

Pieces of wallboard or oilcloth, about 12" x 18", will fit into the case and can be used to turn a pew into a working surface. They can represent a stove or tea table top, or be used for drawing or working with clay. If the floor can be used, an old sheet will take care of the matter of cleanliness when seating the children there for story time; if it is too cold, supplies can be put away and the pews used. The teacher can use the suitcase surface as a place to put her own equipment, covering it with a cloth if that seems better.

Aside from this basic equipment the following equipment travels in the suitcase:

Bible	teaching pictures	small vase
doll bedding	plastic dishes and pans	crayons
construction paper	clay	paste
scissors	masking tape	pencils
books	small folding easel to display pictures	

A few wooden puzzles and blocks, if there is room. Block play figures (see page 85) are always helpful. Pieces of cloth for "dress up" clothes can also be added.

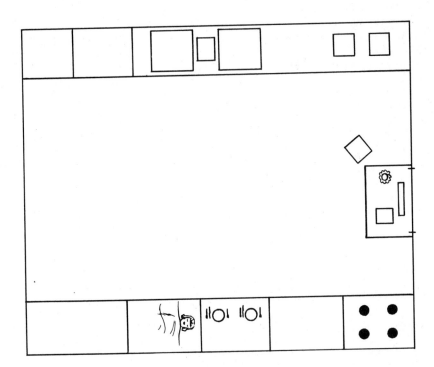

WORK MATERIALS

While it has not been the purpose of this book to give the "how" of the program use of equipment, it might be helpful to share certain basic recipes for activities and other helpful hints that have come from long usage.

Clay

An inexpensive modeling substance:
    1 cup salt
    1 cup cornstarch (flour will work just as well)
    1 cup water

Mix the above ingredients in the top of a double boiler and cook until they form a thick lump about the spoon. Stir constantly. Remove from stove and cool until it can be handled. Dust your hands with flour or cornstarch and knead the mixture until it is smooth and of an even texture; then roll it in a ball and wrap in oiled paper, or put in a plastic bag. In an airtight container it will keep several weeks if put in a refrigerator when not in use for several days. Modeled figures should be allowed to dry and may then be painted with water color. (Modeled figures are apt to deteriorate if kept in a damp place, because of the salt in them.) Water colors or cake coloring may be added to the clay while mixing it to make it attractive for the children. Have very little liquid in the coloring when adding it. This is a very clean type of clay, and will not harm the children if eaten, although they aren't apt to like this much salt! Of course, those who have "clay banks" near them will be able to use natural clay at no cost.

Another good modeling substance is wallpaper cleaner.

Salt Dough

Use: 2 cups flour
      1 cup salt

Mix salt and flour together and add enough water to make the ingredients stick together. The dough will be about the consistency of pie crust dough. Dough may be colored with powdered tempera paint or cake coloring. It is good for modeling by younger children, if there is no reason to keep the result, for it does not harden as quickly or effectively as the other clay. This dough is especially good to use in the housekeeping corner for making cookies or other articles. Kept in a plastic bag in the refrigerator, it may be used over and over again for a long period of time.

Paste

To make one quart of paste, mix 1 cup of white flour with 1/2 cup of cold water; add 4 cups of boiling water; cool for five minutes. Beat until entirely cool. Or use wallpaper paste powder, adding water to proper consistency. In a tightly covered jar this will keep fresh for two weeks or more. Add water if it dries.

Finger Paint

Four tablespoons of dry powdered wallpaper paste; add water to mix to the consistency of liquid paste. Add 1 tablespoon of poster paint to give color. Make I/2 pint. Keep in screw-top jars.

Collage (a fascinating, inexpensive kindergarten activity)

Collage (ko-lazh) is pasting bits of paper or odds and ends on a background sheet of paper to make a picture or design. The odds and ends may be:

bits of cloth	gummed labels
soda straws	buttons
twigs	wood shavings
grasses	sand
sawdust	ribbon
absorbent cotton	yarn, string

Scraps of colored papers cut in various shapes, from adver-tisements in magazines, cellophane, crepe paper, wallpaper

Give the children paste, kindergarten scissors, and a sheet of Manilla or other heavy paper on which to make the picture, and let them use their imaginations! They should work on newspapers or oilcloth at a table or on the floor. Furnish wet rags or towels to wipe sticky fingers!

Masking Tape

Such tape is useful in countless ways in the church school. It is especially good to hold pictures or other articles to the wall, since it will not mar a smooth surface such as the front or back of a good picture. It will stick to most walls. It does not stick long to rough plaster walls (and neither does anything else). It can be purchased at most drug, paint, variety, or hardware stores.

Powdered Tempera Paint

This is an invaluable part of the equipment of the church school. It is used for all kinds of painting at easels, spatter painting, posters, etc. It is used to color salt dough, clay, and finger paint--and in almost any way color can be used. Powdered tempera may be pur-chased at any school supply store, including many bookstores. It is well to make sure the colors are strong--sometimes they are not in the cheaper varieties. Have on hand white, black, and the primary colors (blue, red, yellow). This will represent an invest-ment of several dollars, since this paint cannot often be purchased in less than pound cans. However, since only enough is mixed for immediate use, the supply will keep indefinitely.

In mixing the paint, put powdered tempera into a jar (if you've never mixed paints before, start with about 3 tablespoons of paint); add water slowly, stirring all the while, until the paint is the con-sistency of light cream. Be sure all lumps are out--this sometimes takes quite a bit of stirring. If the paint dries between times of use, add more water--it never need be thrown away, if kept in airtight screw-top jars.

Inexpensive Plants
  Sometimes we neglect to have growing things in the Sunday church school because they cost too much, or there is no one to care for them. The tops of root vegetables, such as carrots, turnips, beets, may be put into water and will again grow lovely greenery. Lentils and other seeds (including grass and rye) may be sprinkled on a sponge that is set in water and will grow a feathery top. The sweet potato makes a lovely plant. If the water container is large enough, all these things can be left a week without care. Ivy and other foliage plants will grow well in water too.